WHAT MUST I DO TO INHERIT ETERNAL LIFE?

*May the Lord
bless you and
keep you.*

WHAT MUST I DO TO INHERIT ETERNAL LIFE?

CLIFFORD ONLEY

HighWay
A division of Anomalos Publishing House
Crane

HighWay

A division of Anomalos Publishing House, Crane 65633

© 2008 by Clifford Onley

All rights reserved. Published 2008

Printed in the United States of America

08 1

ISBN-10: 0981764339

EAN-13: 9780981764337

Cover illustration and design by Steve Warner

Unless otherwise indicated, all scripture quotations are taken from the King James Version of the Bible.

A CIP catalog record for this book is available from the Library of Congress.

To Amy Loudell Onley

CONTENTS

PREFACE

THE BOSS OF heaven and earth gave me this commission, "Go to denominational churches and preach this message: 'Get in the boat, or get out!'" My reaction was, "Sounds great! Let's do it."

Then the Lord let me know that I was to be an evangelist. This led me to struggle with what I thought it meant to be an evangelist. I thought that an evangelist was aimed primarily at those who were not churchgoers. How could I have the direction to go to church people?

One day the Lord said, "The church is a lost and dying world!" In my mind, this was a very dramatic statement. How could the church be a lost and dying world?

Then the Lord began to build this overwhelming desire in me to know the answer to the question: "What must I do to inherit eternal life?" This book is the product of a very long and intense Holy Spirit-directed Bible study of this subject. This caused me to emphatically believe that many, if not most, church people are on a path that leads straight to hell. This book will not only make you aware of what is required of everyone to see the Lord, but it will give you indicators that will let you know what path you are on.

ACKNOWLEDGMENTS

IF MY WIFE of thirty-six years, Mary Ann, and our four children, Stephanie, Amanda, C. J., and Josh, do not obtain eternal life, it will not be because of a lack of knowledge of the truth. I have bombarded them for over twenty years with the revelations that are contained in this book. There is not a single part that they have not been forced to endure hearing continually throughout their lives.

As the Lord taught me, I pounded it into their heads. I learned tremendous things at their expense. As we teach, we are forced to meditate on the subject that we are teaching. The result is that the picture becomes clearer and clearer. Needless to say, it is more fun to preach when you have a captive audience.

The depth of my beautiful wife and children's patience and support cannot be measured. My love for them grows every day.

CHAPTER ONE

THE GREAT AND TERRIBLE DAY OF THE LORD

SO MANY PEOPLE! This must be every person who ever lived, and even those who died before they were born. They are all here. Every color, size, and nationality of the descendents of Adam are all in one place at the same time. Billions and billions of people are all present and must give an answer. It is such a massive group, and they are all waiting their turn to stand before the judge. He is dividing them into two groups.

> And before him shall be gathered all nations: and he shall separate them one from another, as a shepherd divideth his sheep from the goats: And he shall set the sheep on his right hand, but the goats on the left. Then shall the King say unto them on his right hand, Come, ye blessed of my Father, inherit the kingdom prepared for you from the foundation of the world...Then shall he say also unto them on the left hand, Depart from me, ye cursed, into everlasting fire, prepared for the devil and his angels.
>
> MATTHEW 25:32-34, 41

How long will it be before it is my turn to stand before the judge? There goes another one pleading, screaming, and crying.

Such terrible screaming and sobbing! I have never heard anything like it. I wonder what they all did to be treated this way.

These people must have been vicious murderers or something equally horrible. I mean, to be talked to like that and to be carried away crying and moaning that way. They are all pleading and begging, then crying out while they are being carried away.

It sounds like they are yelling about how they always gave money to the church or charities. I think that I heard some saying that they taught Sunday school or were an elder of the church. That guy is yelling something about how he went on mission trips and even cast demons out of people in Jesus' name. They all seem to be saying what they did in the church, or for other people.

Here comes another one. There goes another one begging that the book might be checked again for his name. What did he say? Did he scream something about how his name has to be in the book? There are so many people. What did they do that was so wrong? Do they really deserve this?

Hey, I know that guy! He went to my church for what seems like forever. He was so faithful. He almost never missed. He was Sunday school superintendent and an elder of the church. He really was a nice guy. He owned a hardware store. Why are they dragging him away? What did he do that was so wrong?

That guy worked at the bank. He sure was a nice guy and very successful, too. He approved a loan so I could buy my first car. He was involved in local civic organizations. He did a lot of good for a lot of people. What could he have done that was so terrible?

I sure do not understand this—all of these good people being treated like this! Oh, I knew that guy. He sure was weird. Why is he so happy? Why is he approved while all of these good people are being condemned?

That is my favorite uncle up there now. I sure loved him. He would do anything for you. He would give you the shirt off his back.

Wait! Stop! This is just not right! He was a good man. I know that he was a good man. He went to church all of his life. He did not drink or take dope. He did not run around on his wife. He worked hard. I know that he did not go around doing bad things. This is just not right! Something is wrong here.

I know that he believed in Jesus and was baptized. I do not understand what is going on here. This is just crazy.

That is my pastor up there now. He was a man of God if there ever was one. He taught us so much about the grace and mercy of God. I really cannot believe that they are leading him away like that.

What does it take around here anyway? I mean, the best people I know are being led off screaming and sobbing. How can this be happening?

That lake is so terrible, and they are all screaming in agony! I thought that God was a loving and forgiving God. What happened to the mercy and the grace? How could He send all these good people, even preachers, to that terrible place? They are being cast in by the billions! What happened?

What determines where we will spend eternity is the most important information that anyone could possibly possess. Many people have many ideas about this subject. The number of different ideas just within so-called Christianity is absolutely astounding. Many people prefer to avoid the subject altogether.

A young man in a fifth grade Sunday school class asked me one day, "We worship God, but some people worship the devil. How do we know who is right?" The Lord gave me an answer on the spot.

I held up my thumb and index finger about three inches apart and said, "I say that this is about an inch. What do you say?" He answered, holding his thumb and index finger about an inch apart, "No, this is about an inch."

I said, "How are we going to find out who is right?" He replied, "We need a ruler." I picked up my Bible and said, "Here is your ruler. If you do not know what the ruler says, then you do not know who is right."

Our source for truth on this subject will be our Bible, just as in the days of the great reformers of the Christian church, who declared that the scriptures are the standard for Christian truth. In John 17:17 Jesus declared, "Sanctify them through thy truth: thy word is truth."

On what do you base your ideas? Do you really care enough to lay aside your ideas and what you have been taught to study this subject very objectively? Or will you be one of those who Amos talks about?

Amos 5:18–20 states: "Woe unto you that desire the day of the Lord! To what end is it for you? The day of the Lord is darkness, and not light. As if a man did flee from a lion, and a bear met him; or went into the house, and leaned his hand on the wall, and a serpent bit him. Shall not the day of the Lord be darkness, and not light? even very dark, and no brightness in it?"

In John 8, Jesus speaks to those Jews who believed in Him, and told them this: "Ye are of your father the devil..." (John 8:44). Just being a person who longs to see Jesus will not get you there, and just being one who believed in Him will not get you into heaven.

We must study this subject from God's Word to discover what a descendant of Adam must do to inherit eternal life. A lot of people who think that they know the way to eternal life are bound straight for hell.

Matthew 7:21–23 states: "Not every one that saith unto me, Lord, Lord, shall enter into the kingdom of heaven; but he that doeth the will of my Father which is in heaven. Many will say to me in that day, Lord, Lord, have we not prophesied in thy name? and in thy name have cast out devils? and in thy name done many wonderful works? And then will I profess unto them, I never knew you: depart from me, ye that work iniquity."

When did He say that He knew them? He said, "I never knew you." Many people who prophesy, or preach, in Jesus' name will hear this statement on that day. Many people who have done many wonderful works in Jesus' name will hear this statement on that day. Many people who have even cast out devils will hear this statement on that day: "I never knew you."

One day the Lord said to me, "The Church is a lost and dying world." He had to teach me how that could be true.

CHAPTER TWO

SEARCHING FOR THE
WAY TO LIFE

IN RETROSPECT, I can see how the Lord began to build a desire in me to know what we must do to inherit eternal life. I came to the place where I began to study the Bible to find the answer. I read here and there until one day the Lord said to me, "Study the eighth chapter of Romans."

As I began to study this chapter, I discovered that the last ten words of the first verse were not in all versions of the New Testament. In fact, in my Scofield Bible, I found where it said that these words were "interpolated." I was not familiar with this word. I checked my dictionary and found that it means that these words were added by the translator to aid the understanding of the reader.

The same ten words, "Who walk not after the flesh, but after the Spirit," are in the fourth verse in all versions that I checked. These ten words are very important, because they identify those who are "in Christ." The chapter goes on to amplify who is "in Christ."

Paul goes on to say that those who are "after the flesh" either mind or take care of the things of the flesh, but those who are "after the Spirit," or are "in Christ," either mind or take care of the things of the Spirit.

Jesus summed this up in Matthew 6:31–34:

> Therefore take no thought, saying, What shall we eat? or, What shall we drink? Wherewithal shall we be clothed? (For after all these things do the Gentiles seek:) for your heavenly Father knoweth that ye have need of all these things. But seek ye first the kingdom of God, and his righteousness; and all these things shall be added unto you. Take therefore no thought for the morrow: for the morrow shall take thought for the things of itself. Sufficient unto the day is the evil thereof.

This was Jesus' way of saying that those who are after the Spirit will mind the things of the Spirit. The thing that gives us the ability to do this is faith in the Father. We cannot serve anyone whom we do not trust.

We must trust our employer to pay us in order to serve him or her by doing what he or she asks us to do. If we do not trust them, we will demand payment in advance of providing the service. In other words, we will only work for them if they pay before we work. Likewise, we cannot serve the Lord unless we honestly trust Him to provide everything that we need.

The thing that prevents us from living this way is a lack of trust in God. Then we are part of the group that Jesus addresses in Matthew 6:30, "O ye of little faith."

But for me, the ability to see these things came gradually. After I had been studying the eighth chapter of Romans for a while, I heard a man say that each time you read a "therefore," back up and see what it is there for. In other words, this word indicates a conclusion that is drawn from previously stated facts. So I backed up and studied the sixth and seventh chapters of Romans to better understand the foundation for the eighth chapter.

Then my study began to include more and more of the New Testament. After weeks of this, I sat down one day with a pen and paper and wrote more than sixty pages of what the Lord was teaching me about this subject. Next we will begin to look at what He taught me.

CHAPTER THREE

FIRST STEP ON THE WAY

JESUS SAID, "I AM the way, the truth, and the life: no man cometh unto the Father, but by me" (John 14:6). The Father is the Creator or the source of all life. If Jesus is the only way to the Father, we must follow Jesus to reach the source of all life. Everything that has life, except God, has an obvious beginning. This means that nothing else even competes to be recognized as the source of all life.

Paul said that all of creation testifies to God's existence (Romans 1:20). In other words, the size and magnificence of creation display the scope and lack of limits to the power of God. The more we learn of the complexities of creation, the more we ought to have appreciation for the work of His hands.

Everything in creation has an expected end of physical life at some point, including the sun, unless God intervenes. Solomon said that the grave awaits the wise man and the fool (Ecclesiastes 2:16).

But the New Testament records the witness of many people who saw Jesus after He was raised from the dead with an immortal body by the power of God. He ate and drank after He was raised from the dead, yet He passed through walls and had the ability to translate from one place to another.

As Paul states, we do not desire to be without a body, but to have an immortal one (2 Corinthians 5:1–4). Jesus' body was not found in the tomb, but it was raised an immortal body by the power of Him who created the universe. If we desire the same, we should look to the One who has received one already. We should follow His instructions as to the way to receive life eternal.

What is required to become a follower or disciple of Jesus?

> Then said Jesus unto his disciples, If any man will come after me, let him deny himself, and take up his cross, and follow me. For whosoever will save his life shall lose it: and whosoever will lose his life for my sake shall find it. For what is a man profited, if he shall gain the whole world, and lose his own soul? or what shall a man give in exchange for his soul? For the Son of man shall come in the glory of his Father with his angels; and then he shall reward every man according to his works.
>
> MATTHEW 16:24–27

These conditions apply to anyone who desires to become a follower or disciple of Jesus. He said "any man" and "whosoever," which includes all of us. According to Webster, a disciple is one who accepts and assists in spreading the doctrines of another.

So many people want to accept and assist in spreading what they believe to be the doctrines of Christ, but many of them have not met the conditions that Jesus established as a requirement for becoming a disciple of Christ. They have not lost their life for His sake. In their heart and mind their life is their own.

First Corinthians 6:19–20 states: "What? know ye not that your body is the temple of the Holy Ghost which is in you, which ye have of God, and ye are not your own? For ye are bought with a price: therefore glorify God in your body, and in your spirit, which are God's."

Losing your life for Jesus' sake is the price for becoming a disciple of Christ. Acts 11:26 tells us, "And the disciples were called Christians first in Antioch." Therefore, a true Christian is a disciple of Christ and has become a bond slave to Jesus. If you have given your life to Jesus, you are God's property. But Jesus warned us to decide if we are able to meet these conditions before we start; otherwise, we should not even try to be a disciple of Christ.

> And there went great multitudes with him: and he turned, and said unto them, If any man come to me, and hate not his father, and mother, and wife, and children, and brethren, and sisters, yea, and his own life also, he cannot be my disciple. And whosoever doth not bear his cross, and come after me, cannot be my disciple. For which of you, intending to build a tower, sitteth not down first, and counteth the cost, whether he have sufficient to finish it? Lest haply, after he hath laid the foundation, and is not able to finish it, all that behold it begin to mock him, Saying, This man began to build, and was not able to finish.
>
> LUKE 14:25-30

To the multitudes of would-be followers of Christ today (so-called Christians), the message is the same. Have you counted the cost? Are you willing to surrender anything and everything just to know Him so that you will not be counted among those who hear, "I never knew you: depart from me…" (Matthew 7:23).

What is more important to you than knowing Jesus? Anything can be more valuable to you if you make it more important than following Him.

If we do not surrender complete control of our lives to Jesus,

He will plainly inform us that He never knew us. We must decide if we are willing to go only where He wants us to go, and do only what He wants us to do.

What motivates you to do the things that you do now? Are you making a living? After all, Paul said, "For even when we were with you, this we commanded you, that if any would not work, neither should he eat" (2 Thessalonians 3:10). Becoming a Christian is not for allowing us to be lazy or to just do what we feel like doing. It is to set us free to follow whatever direction for our individual lives that the Lord may give. Then we can make ourselves available for service in the kingdom of heaven. We can say like the apostle Paul, "Lord, what wilt thou have me to do?" (Acts 9:6).

Whatever motivates us to do what we do is our God.

Philippians 3:18–19 states: "(For many walk, of whom I have told you often, and now tell you even weeping, that they are the enemies of the cross of Christ: Whose end is destruction, whose God is their belly, and whose glory is in their shame, who mind earthly things.)"

Those, even within the church, who are motivated to do what they do in order to provide food for their stomach, are bound for hell. Their glory is in their standard of living or how much money they make. Paul declares that this is their shame.

To "mind earthly things" is to take care of the things that pertain to this life in our body. To mind spiritual things is take care of the things that affect our eternal destiny.

Matthew 6:19–21 states: "Lay not up for yourselves treasures upon earth, where moth and rust doth corrupt, and where thieves break through and steal: But lay up for yourselves treasures in heaven, where neither moth nor rust doth corrupt, and where thieves do not break through nor steal: For where your treasure is, there will your heart be also."

The bottom line is that if the things of this world are of much value to you, they become your treasure and consume your heart—and there are a lot of things to feast your eyes on in our world today. Then we begin to desire them just like Eve, who saw that the fruit was pleasant to look at and she began to desire it. Any desirable thing we begin to put our focus on begins to capture our heart.

For the most part, advertising is aimed at creating a desire in us for whatever product or service is being advertised. Advertisers hope to present their product or service in such a way as to make it a god to people and make them say, "Gotta have it." Jesus has an answer about what will happen to you based on where you put your focus.

Matthew 6:22–23 says, "The light of the body is the eye: if therefore thine eye be single, thy whole body shall be full of light. But if thine eye be evil, thy whole body shall be full of darkness. If therefore the light that is in thee be darkness, how great is that darkness!"

If your focus is on the treasures of this life, your whole life is full of darkness. Anything can be treasure to you. As the saying goes, "One man's trash is another man's treasure." The value that you give it in your heart determines whether it is trash or treasure to you.

The apostle Paul establishes what happened to the treasures in his life when he gave his life to Christ:

> But what things were gain to me, those I counted loss for Christ. Yea doubtless, and I count all things but loss for the excellency of the knowledge of Christ Jesus my Lord: for whom I have suffered the loss of all things, and do count them but dung, that I may win Christ, And be found in him, not having mine own righteousness, which is of the law, but that

which is through the faith of Christ, the righteousness which is of God by faith: That I may know him, and the power of his resurrection, and the fellowship of his sufferings, being made conformable unto his death; If by any means I might attain unto the resurrection of the dead.

PHILIPPIANS 3:7–11

Are you willing to lose everything that is important to you, including your family, or even your own life, to know Christ Jesus? Remember, in Luke 15 Jesus said that if you hold anything back, you cannot be His disciple. Will you count everything that is important to you "dung" compared to knowing Christ Jesus? That includes your earthly life. How important is attaining eternal life to you?

Following this path is the only way to become a true Christian. The pretenders will all hear, "I never knew you: depart from me, ye that work iniquity" (Matthew 7:23). Which will you be—a pretender or a true disciple of Christ?

Jesus continues on the subject of who you belong to in Matthew 6:24. "No man can serve two masters: for either he will hate the one, and love the other; or else he will hold to the one, and despise the other. Ye cannot serve God and mammon."

This is a no-holds-barred truth. You cannot seek God and things or money. If you spend your time and focus seeking things, power, position, or money, you are not seeking God. If you are seeking God, you are not seeking things, power, position, or money. Whom do you serve?

Remember the question that Jesus asked in Matthew 16:26: "For what is a man profited, if he shall gain the whole world, and lose his own soul? or what shall a man give in exchange for his soul?" For what will you sell your soul? Remember, Jesus was offered the whole world for His soul.

Matthew 4:8–10 states: "Again, the devil taketh him up into an exceeding high mountain, and sheweth him all the kingdoms of the world, and the glory of them; And saith unto him, All these things will I give thee, if thou wilt fall down and worship me. Then saith Jesus unto him, Get thee hence, Satan: for it is written, Thou shalt worship the Lord thy God, and him only shalt thou serve."

Whom or what do you serve? What dictates where you go and what you do? No man can serve two masters. Have you counted the cost? Will you give everything and count it but dung? How much is your eternal soul worth?

The first step on the way to life is to enter at the straight gate, which is giving yourself to Christ Jesus, holding nothing back. Have you lost your life for His sake?

Have you denied yourself, or are you still meditating on what you want? Have you buried your dreams and visions to take up Jesus' dreams and visions for your life?

Have you taken up your cross? Have you said, "Lord, if I die, I die, but I will still serve you to the end"? Have you settled it with yourself that even your life on this earth is not worth keeping if the price is eternity in hell? As Jesus asked, "What will you gain if you gain the whole world, then die and go to hell?" (Matthew 16:26).

Have you begun to follow Jesus? Are you living in His words? Are you studying them and meditating on them day and night?

John 8:31–32 says, "Then said Jesus to those Jews which believed on him, If ye continue in my word, then are ye my disciples indeed; And ye shall know the truth, and the truth shall make you free."

What makes you a disciple of Christ is doing what He said. You cannot do what He said if you do not know what He said. To really know what He said, you have to study His words intensely until you know them.

Jesus told the Sadducees that bad doctrine comes from not knowing the scriptures and/or not knowing the power of God. You can know from creation that the power of God is without limit. It is far beyond being measurable.

As mankind learns more and more about creation, the complexity of God's work becomes more apparent. The more we learn, the more we realize how much we do not know. Many scientific theories that seek to explain creation do not even last fifty years before they are proven wrong these days, yet we are supposed to believe that all this happened by accident?

Then there are real present-day miracles that the Spirit of God performs all over the world. Once I was relating to someone I worked with that I had seen an arm grow while someone was praying. This person said that they would like to see something like that. I told him that a person has to go where people believe in miracles to see them. In other words, you have to go where people pray and believe to see God respond with an obvious intervention in the physical world.

Joshua was a man who knew the power of God. He was in Egypt when God brought all the plagues on the Egyptians to make a reputation for Himself in the world as being a mighty deliverer (Romans 9:17). The Lord's instruction to Joshua came in Joshua 1:8: "This book of the law shall not depart out of thy mouth; but thou shalt meditate therein day and night, that thou mayest observe to do according to all that is written therein: for then thou shalt make thy way prosperous, and then thou shalt have good success."

The secret to living in accordance with God's Word is to keep speaking it and to meditate on it day and night. This is the exact same instruction that Jesus gave in John 8:31–32. The apostle Paul gives the same instruction with the same expected outcome in Romans.

Romans 12:1–2 states: "I beseech you therefore, brethren, by the mercies of God, that ye present your bodies a living sacrifice, holy, acceptable unto God, which is your reasonable service. And be not conformed to this world: but be ye transformed by the renewing of your mind, that ye may prove what is that good, and acceptable, and perfect, will of God."

We gain the ability to show the world what God desires for a person's life to be by having the way that we think changed by God's Word. Just hearing it once or twice does not change the way we think. We have to live in it and meditate on it day and night. In other words, there cannot be a time where God's Word is not controlling what we think, say, and do. Then God's will for our lives will be done for all to see.

Knowing the power of God is what gives us the ability to put God's instruction into practice in our lives. It gives us the ability to trust Him. True trust in anyone is developed only in a close relationship where that person demonstrates their trustworthiness. Therefore, trust in God is built on the history of His actions as recorded in the Holy Bible and our own personal experiences with Him.

Real trust is always the product of a close relationship in which people prove themselves to be trustworthy. This does not happen in thirty minutes or less. It takes time, but the more intimate the relationship, the quicker a real trusting relationship can develop.

An intimate relationship with God involves keeping His word in your mouth and meditating on it day and night. It also involves learning to hear His voice, and it involves a lot of prayer. An intimate relationship comes only when there are no secrets between the two parties and everything is subject to discussion. There are no subjects that are off limits. An intimate relationship with God is closer than any other, because you know that you have no secrets from God. There is nothing about you that He does not already know.

Jesus' trust in the Father was tested many times. His faith was tested on the mount of temptation. His faith was tested by demons and people on many occasions that are recorded in the gospels. And finally, His faith was tested by the cross.

First, on the mount of temptation, He was tested with the lust of the flesh, the lust of the eyes, and the pride of life. The lust of the flesh was when, at the point of starvation, He was told to command the stones to be made bread. Then the lust of the eyes was to be offered all the kingdoms of the world and the glory of them. The pride of life was to cast Himself down from the highest point of the temple because, after all, He is the Son of God. His lust and pride were found to be completely crucified.

His faith was such that He feared neither demons nor people. He commanded the spirits with His word, and when His disciples pointed out to Him that the Jews had desired to stone Him, He stated that He would not slip around in the dark, but He would go to raise Lazarus in broad daylight.

Although He dreaded the cross to the point where He could even wish for death, He submitted Himself to the Father's will.

Matthew 26:37–39 states: "And he took with him Peter and the two sons of Zebedee, and began to be sorrowful and very heavy. Then saith he unto them, My soul is exceeding sorrowful, even unto death: tarry ye here, and watch with me. And he went a little farther, and fell on his face, and prayed, saying, O my Father, if it be possible, let this cup pass from me: nevertheless not as I will, but as thou wilt."

Have you ever dreaded anything so much that your sweat was beyond control, and you could have wished for death rather than endure what was ahead of you? This was how much Jesus dreaded what was ahead of Him. But even on the cross, He said, "Father, into thy hands I commend my spirit" (Luke 23:46). When He voluntarily surrendered His spirit, He entrusted it to the Father. Thereby He trusted that the Father would protect and preserve His spirit. We also must trust the Father to ensure our eternal destiny, believing that He will keep His word.

In Philippians 2:5–8 Paul advises us to have the attitude that Jesus had: "Let this mind be in you, which was also in Christ Jesus: Who, being in the form of God, thought it not robbery to be equal with God: But made himself of no reputation, and took upon him the form of a servant, and was made in the likeness of men: And being found in fashion as a man, he humbled himself, and became obedient unto death, even the death of the cross."

Jesus, being in heaven and believing that it took nothing away from the Father for Him to be His son, willingly became a descendant of Adam. He gave up His reputation of being equal with God and was born into a poor and, up until then, insignificant family from Nazareth. To anyone who suggested that Jesus might be the Christ, the Pharisees replied, "Search, and look: for out of Galilee ariseth no prophet" (John 7:52). Then the Son of God, who made Himself so insignificant, became obedient, even to death on the cross. Likewise, we should make ourselves insignificant in our own eyes and become obedient even unto death.

If we do not become obedient, obeying all of Jesus' instructions, 1 John 2:4 is very clear: "He that saith, I know him, and keepeth not his commandments, is a liar, and the truth is not in him." Have you denied yourself, taken up your cross, and begun to follow Jesus, or are you a liar?

Jesus taught a parable that identifies the reasons why His words will or will not have the desired effect on your life. Next we will examine this parable.

CHAPTER FOUR

GOOD GROUND?

WHEN I GAVE my life to Jesus, I did not eat and only slept about three hours a night for the first three days. I have never had such incredible joy and peace. I prayed from about midnight until about three o'clock in the morning those three nights. I was working about ten or eleven hours a day as the manager of a fuel and farm supply business. I never set out to not eat or sleep. I just was not hungry or tired. After three days, I realized that I had not eaten since Sunday. When I mentioned that I had not eaten in three days, some family members became very worried about me, so I began to eat and sleep more, but the peace and joy remained.

I began to very hungrily read the Word of God. I just could not get enough of it. I carried my Bible with me everywhere. Every available minute I spent reading the Word of God. Then I got some preaching tapes. I carried them with me everywhere and listened to them hour after hour after hour. If there were six tapes in a series, I would listen to them in order at least nine times each in a three-day period.

After about the first two weeks, my brother-in-law, with whom

I had been very close, looked at me and said, "I don't know you anymore." I was a changed person. I did not say the same things anymore. I did not think the same things anymore. I did not do the same things anymore. I was a new person.

Then the Lord directed us to move to Tulsa, Oklahoma, for me to attend Oral Roberts University. This move was accomplished by one miracle of God after another. We had four small children and a lot of stuff. We ran a garage sale for a month, selling things very cheap, and we still had a lot of stuff.

Five days before we were scheduled to leave town, we did not have nearly enough resources to afford the move, but we continued to prepare to move. Then the Lord provided much more than we needed just four days before we were to leave.

We arrived in Tulsa with four small children and my nephew with no place to live and no jobs. We faced many trials and difficulties, but the Lord delivered us from them all.

We still are faced with the same things that other people are faced with that can cause the Word of God to fail to produce the desired fruit in their lives. As long as we are alive and remain, we all will have opportunities to be overcome or led away by these things. Let's take a look at some of the things that can prevent us from entering at the straight gate or continuing down the narrow path that leads to life.

> And he spake many things unto them in parables, saying, Behold, a sower went forth to sow; And when he sowed, some seeds fell by the way side, and the fowls came and devoured them up: Some fell upon stony places, where they had not much earth: and forthwith they sprung up, because they had no deepness of earth: And when the sun was up, they were scorched; and because they had no root, they withered away. And some

fell among thorns; and the thorns sprung up, and choked them: But other fell into good ground, and brought forth fruit, some an hundredfold, some sixtyfold, some thirtyfold. Who hath ears to hear, let him hear.

MATTHEW 13:3-9

This parable teaches why the Word of God does not produce the result that it is designed to produce in many people's lives. Just because we receive instruction or correction does not mean that it will produce the intended results in our lives. The instruction must be mixed with faith and be put into practice for it to produce the results.

After everyone left, the disciples asked Jesus why He taught the people in parables. He said that it was given to the disciples to know the mysteries of the kingdom of heaven, but that it was not given to the others to know them.

Then He said, "For whosoever hath, to him shall be given, and he shall have more abundance: but whosoever hath not, from him shall be taken away even that he hath" (Matthew 13:12). Those who have an understanding of the foundation of Christianity that has been amplified in the beginning of this book, have the ability to see and perceive more of the truths in God's Word.

If you do not have a good understanding of the foundation, your whole belief system may be built on a bad foundation, which can cause the whole thing to be wrong. In other words, if you do not understand the true principles on which it is founded, how could you really understand anything that is built on that foundation?

Jesus asked in Mark 4:13, "And he said unto them, Know ye not this parable? and how then will ye know all parables?" In other words, if you do not understand this parable, how will you understand any parable? This parable teaches a basic understanding of how God's Word works.

Matthew 13:18–19 states: "Hear ye therefore the parable of the sower. When any one heareth the word of the kingdom, and understandeth it not, then cometh the wicked one, and catcheth away that which was sown in his heart. This is he which receiveth seed by the way side."

The devil is able to steal the Word that is sown in a person's heart when he or she does not understand it. Is it because the message is too complicated for some people to understand? If so, why did He say that we must become as little children to enter the kingdom of heaven? And why did He say, "I thank thee, O Father, Lord of heaven and earth, because thou hast hid these things from the wise and prudent, and hast revealed them unto babes"? (Matthew 11:25).

Jesus had already said why they could not understand the message. It was because their hearts had become calloused and hard, and they had closed their eyes so they could not understand. The last line of the parable states, "Who hath ears to hear, let him hear" (Matthew 13:9). This was not a question of who had ears on their head or who had the ability to hear sound waves. This was a question of whose spiritual heart was soft and open enough to receive and perceive what Jesus was teaching.

Is your spiritual heart soft or are you hard-hearted? A hard heart is the result of sin in a person's life for which he has not repented. This means that he continues doing things that are not right in God's sight. When evil rules a person's life, he becomes hard-hearted. When we first start doing something that we know is wrong in God's sight, our conscience convicts us. When we continue to do those things anyway, our conscience becomes very hard. Paul said that it becomes like flesh that has been seared over with a hot iron. With time it becomes scarred and unfeeling. People with hearts in this condition cannot receive correction.

> Now we have received, not the spirit of the world, but the spirit which is of God; that we might know the things that are freely given to us of God. Which things also we speak, not in the words which man's wisdom teacheth, but which the Holy Ghost teacheth; comparing spiritual things with spiritual. But the natural man receiveth not the things of the Spirit of God: for they are foolishness unto him: neither can he know them, because they are spiritually discerned.
>
> 1 CORINTHIANS 2:12–14

The hard-hearted person who is without the Spirit of God is not able to understand the mysteries of the kingdom of heaven. He simply does not have the ability, because they are not understood intellectually, but spiritually.

The heart of man is a greater controller of his actions than his mind. Jesus said, "For out of the heart proceed evil thoughts, murders, adulteries, fornications, thefts, false witness, blasphemies" (Matthew 15:19). The mind assesses data and forms conclusions based on the data available. It then directs the body to respond accordingly. But the heart sets the character of a person and causes him to do things of which even he does not approve.

Romans 7:19–21 states, "For the good that I would I do not: but the evil which I would not, that I do. Now if I do that I would not, it is no more I that do it, but sin that dwelleth in me. I find then a law, that, when I would do good, evil is present with me."

An evil heart will overrule the will of a person, causing him to do things that even he does not desire. Then comes the expression, "The devil made me do it." James says, "But every man is tempted, when he is drawn away of his own lust, and enticed" (James 1:14).

Evil lives in the heart of natural man. Therefore, when people have evil thoughts or do evil things, they are acting naturally. To them, the things that a spiritual person does are unnatural and they are unable to understand why a person would do those things. The spiritual man not only has the Spirit to guide him, but also his mind to assess spiritual data and arrive at conclusions based on that data.

Matthew 13:20–21 states: "But he that received the seed into stony places, the same is he that heareth the word, and anon with joy receiveth it; Yet hath he no root in himself, but dureth for a while: for when tribulation or persecution ariseth because of the word, by and by he is offended."

This person hears the Word of the kingdom, understands it, and at once accepts it as God's Word. He then begins to put into practice what he heard. But when trouble or persecution comes to him because of the Word, he decides that it does not work and goes back to his old ways. This is because the Word has not taken root deep in his heart.

Every disciple forsook Jesus when He was arrested. Peter flatly denied knowing Him three times that night. Paul stated that everyone left Him except Luke when it came time for Him to stand before Caesar. Persecution runs off a lot of people. If the Word of God is not deeply rooted in a person's heart, persecution and trouble will cause him to turn from the truth of God's Word.

Paul clearly states, "Yea, and all that will live godly in Christ Jesus shall suffer persecution" (2 Timothy 3:12). Peter declared, "Beloved, think it not strange concerning the fiery trial which is to try you, as though some strange thing happened unto you" (1

Peter 4:12). The persecution is going to come if you try to live godly in Christ Jesus, and it will either destroy the Word in you or strengthen it.

Some farmers want hot, dry weather at certain times in the growing season, because that will cause the plant to put down deeper roots. The plant also will not grow as much stalk above ground for the same reason. Most plants will produce much more fruit if they have a great root system and a smaller plant above ground. That big, visible plant takes a lot of nutrients and water just to keep it alive.

Proper pruning makes for much good fruit. Many Christians have a lot of show, but not much root or fruit.

Jesus said, "Herein is my Father glorified, that ye bear much fruit; so shall ye be my disciples" (John 15:8). If we are true disciples of Jesus, we will bear much fruit of the Spirit. He prunes and disciplines us so that we will bear much good fruit. As we live in His teachings, we are transformed into being like Him.

Matthew 13:22 states: "He also that received seed among the thorns is he that heareth the word; and the care of this world, and the deceitfulness of riches, choke the word, and he becometh unfruitful."

This person hears the Word of the kingdom, understands it, has root in himself, and yet he becomes unfruitful. The devil cannot steal the Word from him. Tribulation and persecution cannot drive it out of him. But he becomes distracted by "making a living" and "seeking the good life" or "the pursuit of happiness."

The distractions occupy his time and attention. He has to take care of his job or business. There are more "nice things" in our world today than ever before in all of history. There are people bombarding us all of the time with how much we need what they have to offer. If they can reach us through any means, they are very busy telling us how much we need what they have. This is all an effort to build lust in our heart so that they can control us with whatever they have. This is lust of the eyes, lust of the flesh, or the pride of life trying to control us. Paul said that he kept his body under subjection so that his natural desires would not control his life (1 Corinthians 9:27).

Matthew 6:19–21 states: "Lay not up for yourselves treasures upon earth, where moth and rust doth corrupt, and where thieves break through and steal: But lay up for yourselves treasures in heaven, where neither moth nor rust doth corrupt, and where thieves do not break through nor steal: For where your treasure is, there will your heart be also."

The value that a person places on anything is what makes it a treasure to him. There is the old expression, "One man's trash is another man's treasure." Another expression is, "Beauty is in the eye of the beholder." The point is that anything may or may not be treasure to anyone. Anything that is treasure to you will have your heart. What is most valuable to you? Is it money, houses, jewelry, cars, power, or any number of things that the people of this world have deemed to have value? What do you desire? Is it the things of this world or the things of God? Whatever gets more of your time and attention is what you will desire. Whatever your eyes are on will hold your affection.

Colossians 3:1–2 states: "If ye then be risen with Christ, seek those things which are above, where Christ sitteth on the right hand of God. Set your affection on things above, not on things on the earth."

Paul states that if you are really a Christian, set your eyes and affection on the things of God, not on things on this earth. Our eyes must be on the things of God for us to have a true desire for more of God. Our hunger for God will be a direct measure of how much our eyes are on the things of God.

Matthew 6:22–24 states: "The light of the body is the eye: if therefore thine eye be single, thy whole body shall be full of light. But if thine eye be evil, thy whole body shall be full of darkness. If therefore the light that is in thee be darkness, how great is that darkness! No man can serve two masters: for either he will hate the one, and love the other; or else he will hold to the one and despise the other. Ye cannot serve God and mammon."

If your attention is locked onto the things of God, your eye is single. If you have set your affection on things above and not on the things of this world, your eye is single. If you really do not care about the things of this world because your attention is fixed on the things of God, your eye is single. But if your affection is set on the things of this world, the light that is in you is darkness. The light of God does not exist in you. It is impossible to seek God and the things of this world. If you really love God, you will despise seeking the things of this world. Whatever motivates us is our god. It has become who or what we serve.

Matthew 6:25 states: "Therefore I say unto you, Take no thought for your life, what ye shall eat, or what ye shall drink; nor for your body, what ye shall put on. Is not the life more than meat, and the body than raiment?"

We cannot serve God and the things of this world simultaneously. Jesus stated that we should not have any anxious thoughts about what we will have to eat, drink, or wear. Now these are our three most basic needs, so why should we not worry about making a living? (Matthew 6:25). After all, did Paul not say that if a man would not work, we should not allow him to eat? (2 Thessalonians 3:10).

Jesus is talking about what motivates us to do what we do. Seeking the kingdom of God in our lives should be our motivation. This means doing only those things that please the Father should be what motivates us. Jesus said, "And he that sent me is with me: the Father hath not left me alone; for I do always those things that please him" (John 8:29). Jesus only did the things that pleased the Father; therefore, the Father never left Him.

If you desire the abiding presence in your life, you must always do the things that please the Father. Isaiah 59:1–2 states: "Behold, the Lord's hand is not shortened, that it cannot save; neither his ear heavy, that it cannot hear: But your iniquities have separated between you and your God, and your sins have hid his face from you, that he will not hear."

When we do things that are not pleasing to God, we create a separation between ourselves and God. Then we must repent and ask for God's forgiveness to restore our relationship with Him. If our eye is not single, we will continually do those things that are not pleasing to God.

Romans 8:5–8 states: "For they that are after the flesh do mind the things of the flesh; but they that after the Spirit the things of the Spirit. For to be carnally minded is death; but to be spiritually minded is life and peace. Because the carnal mind is enmity against God: for it is not subject to the law of God, neither indeed can be. So then they that are in the flesh cannot please God."

Those whose motivation in life is to supply the natural needs and desires of the body—and those things that we desire—cannot please God. The mind that is set on those things is naturally opposed to the law of God. Paul states that it is impossible for the mind that is occupied with supplying natural needs and desires to be subject to the law of God. Those who are motivated by making a living or by pursing the things that they desire cannot please God. This is why Jesus said that we should not have our thoughts on what we will eat or how the rest of our needs will be met.

Jesus stated very clearly that if we will occupy ourselves with seeking God's rule over every part of our lives, God will always take care of us. After all, He made us, and He knows better than we do what we need. His example was that God takes care of the birds, and He provides flowers to dress the earth, so He will much more provide for those who love and obey Him. It is impossible for us to seek God's rule over our lives and seek money and things at the same time.

Does this mean that we do not work at a regular job? Not necessarily. It simply means that we make ourselves subject to God's direction for our lives. The Lord always has a great plan for our lives. This is what motivates us every day.

To obey God, we must honestly trust the Lord to take care of us. If we are employed, we chose to trust the company or the person who employs us. We chose to believe that our employer would pay us what he or she said would be paid to us when we were hired. We applied to subject ourselves to his or her direction, trusting that he or she would pay us in return. We chose him or her to take care of us. If we can choose to trust people that we do not know, why would we not trust Almighty God?

We cannot obey anyone's direction that we do not trust. A man asks us to do a job and promises to pay us. We choose to believe him or we will not obey. Likewise, we cannot obey God Almighty if we do not honestly trust Him. The Lord is accepting applications.

Luke 10:2 states: "Therefore said he unto them, The harvest truly is great, but the labourers are few: pray ye herefore the Lord of the harvest, that he would send forth labourers into his harvest."

Jesus said that we should pray to the Lord that He would send laborers into His harvest. But before He said this, one person came to Jesus and said that he would follow Jesus anywhere Jesus went. Jesus' response was that foxes have a place to sleep, and the birds have a place to sleep, but Jesus had no place of His own. In other words, are you ready for whatever you may have to endure for Jesus' sake?

Then Jesus invited a man to follow Him, to which the man replied that he would like to wait until after he buried his father. Jesus responded, "Let the dead bury their dead: but go thou and preach the kingdom of God" (Luke 9:60).

Another replied that he would follow Jesus, but he desired to go to his house to tell his family goodbye first. Luke 9:62 states: "And Jesus said unto him, No man, having put his hand to the plough, and looking back, is fit for the kingdom of God."

Once again, we see that the price is our life.

Matthew 13:23 states: "But he that received seed into the good ground is he that heareth the word, and understandeth it; which also beareth fruit, and bringeth forth, some an hundred-fold, some sixty, some thirty."

Are you good ground? Is your heart soft so that you can understand the message of the kingdom? Do you trust Almighty God, or will the cares of this life and the deceitfulness of riches prevent the Word about the kingdom from producing fruit in your life?

Will you keep your attention on the Word so it can put roots down deep in your heart so persecution will not prevent it from producing fruit? Is your heart good ground? Will you produce fruit worthy of the kingdom of heaven?

The Lord taught me how we can know if His Word has really produced good fruit in our lives. Next we will look at how we can know for sure.

VITAL SIGNS

A **FEW YEARS AGO,** as I was driving by a hospital, I was meditating on the fact that my "old man," that is, my old life of being controlled by my natural desires, had to die. The Lord asked me, "How do you tell when someone is dead?" I replied, "You check their vital signs." Then He said to me, "The vital signs of the old man are listed in Galatians." I understood that He was speaking about the works of the flesh listed in Galatians 5:19–21. But as to our "old man" dying, Paul describes himself in Galatians 2:20: "I am crucified with Christ: nevertheless I live; yet not I, but Christ liveth in me: and the life which I now live in the flesh I live by the faith of the Son of God, who loved me, and gave himself for me."

Paul declares that his life is not his own, but he has given it to Christ Jesus so that Jesus' life can be lived through him. Likewise, when we give our lives to Jesus, we no longer belong to ourselves. We become God's. The way to know if this has truly happened is found in 2 Corinthians 5:17–18: "Therefore if any man be in Christ, he is a new creature: old things are passed away; behold, all things are become new. And all things are of God…"

If we truly are in Christ, the old things are passed away. This means that we do not think like we did before. We do not speak the same things that we said before. We do not do the same things that we did before. All things have become new, and all things are of God. In other words, if we are truly "in Christ," everything in every area of our life is pleasing to God. What we do is pleasing to God. The things that we say are only things that please God. We bring every thought captive to the obedience of Christ so that even our thoughts are pleasing to God. This only happens if we have totally surrendered our lives to Christ Jesus.

How can we know if we have truly surrendered our life totally to Christ? Paul says, "Examine yourselves, whether ye be in the faith; prove your own selves..." (2 Corinthians 13:5). We can check ourselves for the "vital signs of the old man."

> Now the works of the flesh are manifest, which are these;
> adultery, fornication, uncleanness, lasciviousness, idolatry,
> witchcraft, hatred, variance, emulations, wrath, strife, seditions,
> heresies,envyings, murders, drunkenness, revellings, and such like:
> of the which I tell you before, as I have also told you in time past,
> that they which do such things shall not inherit the kingdom of God.
>
> GALATIANS 5:19–21

Paul declares that people who do these things will not live in the kingdom of heaven. They will spend eternity in the other place known as Hades. This list contains a group of big words, so we will examine them to see exactly what Paul is identifying.

Adultery

You may say, "I would never do that!" Remember that Jesus said, "Ye have heard that it was said by them of old time, Thou shalt not commit adultery: but I say unto you, That whosoever looketh on a woman to lust after her hath committed adultery with her already in his heart" (Mathew 5:27–28).

Some people might not want to take this literally, but the very next verse says, "And if thy right eye offend thee, pluck it out, and cast it from thee: for it is profitable for thee that one of thy members should perish, not that thy whole body should be cast into hell" (Matthew 5:29). Obviously, what you look at can send you to hell.

Jesus said that we would be better off blind than to go to hell because of the things at which we look. This is true if we allow lust to be produced in our heart by the things that hold our attention.

Plucking out your eye is a mighty drastic action. Some people might think that He did not mean this literally. Remember, it is your whole body that will be cast into hell. In Matthew 16, Jesus asked what a man would give in exchange for his soul. Would your sight be too great a price to pay for eternal life?

According to Webster, "adultery" is voluntary sexual intercourse between a married person and anyone other than their mate. According to Jesus, however, adultery is even the desire in a married person for sex with anyone to whom that person is not married.

Adultery, like all other sin, is a spiritual problem and is best treated as such. Many influential people have fallen to this temptation. To rule over this temptation, a person's heart must be changed by the power of God, and that person must keep his body and mind under subjection. In other words, a person must rule over his own thoughts and actions.

Second Corinthians 10:5 says, "Casting down imaginations, and every high thing that exalteth itself against the knowledge of God, and bringing into captivity every thought to the obedience of Christ." Every thought must be held captive to be obedient to the teachings of Jesus. We must put Jesus' words in our mouth to control our thoughts whenever our thoughts are contrary to the teachings of Jesus.

Fornication

Growing up in church I heard the word "fornication," but no one ever said what it meant. In my mind, I imagined that it must be the greatest evil conceivable to man. According to the Word of God, that is not far from being totally correct. Paul said, "Flee fornication. Every sin that a man doeth is without the body; but he that committeth fornication sinneth against his own body" (1 Corinthians 6:18).

According to Webster, "fornication" is human sexual intercourse other than between a man and his wife. There can be no sex or desire for sex other than between a man and his lawful wife. All other sex is fornication and will cause the participant to spend eternity in hell if the fornication, or even the desire for it, does not cease. Those who commit or desire to commit fornication must repent from it.

The Greek word *porneuo* is translated into English as "fornication," and literally means harlotry (including adultery and incest and, figuratively, idolatry). A harlot is a prostitute, and to practice idolatry or to idolize someone is to worship them as a god. As such, this makes a person's god a whore. Flee fornication!

Uncleanness

This is another word that no one explained to me while I was growing up in church. I thought it meant that a person must have

WHAT MUST I DO TO INHERIT ETERNAL LIFE?

gotten something really ugly on themselves. I thought this was a case of just a little dirt behind the ears.

The Greek word *akatharsia* is translated into English as "uncleanness." It means impurity (physically or morally). "Impure" does not necessarily mean highly polluted.

According to Webster, "pure" means free from what vitiates, weakens, or pollutes. It contains nothing that does not properly belong: free from moral fault or guilt. Second Corinthians 5:17 states that all things have become new. To be unclean is to have any moral fault or something that has not been made like God in a person. Jesus said, "Be ye therefore perfect, even as your Father which is in heaven is perfect" (Matthew 5:48).

Lasciviousness

The word "lasciviousness" is so big and sounds so complicated that I could not even guess what it meant. I wondered if there was anyone in the church who really knew what this word meant. I don't remember ever hearing this word in church while I was growing up.

The Greek word for "lasciviousness" is *aselgeia,* which literally means incontinent. According to Webster, "incontinent" means lacking self-restraint, unable to contain, keep, or restrain: uncontrolled. This simply means a lack of self-control. In other words, a person does things of which they do not approve. In Romans 7:15 Paul states, "For that which I do, I allow not: for what I would, that do I not; but what I hate, that do I."

This is identified by Paul as a work of the flesh, and he said, "And they that are Christ's have crucified the flesh with the affections and lusts" (Galatians 5:24). This could not have been describing Paul as a Christian. As the context indicates, this is

41

describing a man under the law. The Galatian letter was written to instruct the Galatians to count themselves dead to the law.

Does this mean that the law is dead? Jesus said that heaven and earth would pass away before one punctuation mark of the law. In Romans 8:4 Paul declares, "That the righteousness of the law might be fulfilled in us, who walk not after the flesh, but after the Spirit." This means that the righteous requirements of the law can be fulfilled in our lives if we are led by the Spirit and not controlled by our natural desires.

Do you have things in your life that control you? Do you continue to do things of which God does not approve? Are you controlled by the things that you naturally desire, like food or sex? Are you controlled by a desire for things that you see or of which you hear? Are you controlled by your pride? To belong to Christ, you must be controlled by the Holy Spirit, not by your natural desires.

This does not necessarily mean that a person kills or steals to provide what they naturally desire. It simply means that they do what they do to provide the necessities of life, and/or the things that they want. Things like food, clothes, housing, utilities, vehicles, toys, or other things that we desire are the things that motivate us to get up and go to work.

Jesus said, "Take no thought for your life, what ye shall eat, or what ye shall drink; nor yet for your body, what ye shall put on" (Matthew 6:25). His reason for saying this is found in Matthew 6:32: "For your heavenly Father knoweth that ye have need of all these things." If we belong to God and we are seeking His rule over our lives, we can expect Him to provide for us. But if our natural desires control us while we claim to be a follower of Christ, we are as the people that Paul speaks of in Philippians 3:18–19: "(For many walk, of whom I have told you often, and now tell you even weeping, that they are the enemies of the cross of Christ: Whose end is destruction, whose God is their belly, and whose glory is in their shame, who mind earthly things.)"

To "mind earthly things" is simply to take care of the things of this life. It is to be motivated by our natural needs. Does this mean that we do not work? God forbid! It means that we are motivated by the desire to please God in everything that we do rather than being motivated by our needs and desires. Paul states very clearly that if we are motivated by our stomach, we are enemies of the cross, whose end is destruction. What motivates you to do what you do? Do you have your affections set on things above, or on things in this world?

Idolatry

The Greek word *eidololatreia* is translated into English as "idolatry," and means image worship. This is not news to most people. Idolatry is not practiced to a great degree in the U.S. However, it was practiced commonly in the places that Paul visited. According to Colossians 3:5, it is not a complete definition of this word: "Mortify therefore your members which are upon the earth; fornication, uncleanness, inordinate affection, evil concupiscence, and covetousness, which is idolatry."

We know that covetousness constitutes idolatry. The Greek word *pleonexia* is translated into English as "covetousness," and means avarice. Webster defines "avarice" as excessive or insatiable desire for wealth or gain. If we allow the desire for things to control our lives, we are idol worshippers. Romans 6:16 states, "Know ye not, that to whom ye yield yourselves servants to obey, his servants ye are to whom ye obey..." Whatever you submit yourself to is your master. Submit yourself to God!

Witchcraft

The Greek word *pharmakeia* is translated into English as "witchcraft." It means medication (pharmacy). When you drove down to the pharmacy, you did not know that you were going to visit the local witchcraft shop. The root word for this is *pharmakon*, and it means a drug or spell-giving potion. You knew that the pharmacy had drugs, even hallucinogens, but you did not think of them as products of witchcraft. Drugs are not the product of witchcraft if they are not used for the purpose of gaining control over another person's life over which you have no right to control. The pharmacist is not dispensing drugs for this purpose.

The dope dealer is practicing witchcraft. His purpose is not simply to benefit those to whom he sells or gives his drugs. He is out to gain control over their lives so that he can benefit by gaining something of value to him. The pharmacist is dispensing his medications for the purpose of making money, but his motive is also to benefit others. The real purpose of witchcraft is to gain power or control.

No one has the right to control the lives of other people, except those who are ordained by God. Parents have a right and responsibility to control the lives of their children until the children are of age. The government has a right to establish organizations for the purpose of exercising some control over its citizens' lives. The police have a right to rule over lawbreakers. Paul said that the man who bears the sword for the punishment of evildoers is the minister of God (Romans 13:3–4).

People use a variety of things to gain control over the lives of others. Drugs, alcohol, intimidation, manipulation, lies, coercion, and a multitude of other things are used for this purpose.

First Samuel 15:23 says, "For rebellion is as the sin of witchcraft, and stubbornness is as iniquity and idolatry..." Webster defines "rebellion" as opposition to one in authority or dominance. To rebel is to act in or show disobedience, to feel or exhibit anger or revulsion. This means that to be disobedient to, or to show anger towards, those whom God has placed in a position of authority over us, is the same as witchcraft. It is like witchcraft in reverse. Instead of desiring to control, it is a failure to submit to God-ordained control over our lives.

Hatred

The Greek word *echthra* is translated into English as "hatred," and implies hostility. Webster defines "hostility" as antagonism, opposition, or resistance in thought or principle.

> Ye have heard that it hath been said, An eye for an eye, and a tooth for a tooth: But I say unto you, That ye resist not evil: but whosoever shall smite thee on thy right cheek, turn to him the other also. And if any man will sue thee at law, and take away thy coat, let him have thy cloak also. And whosoever shall compel thee to go a mile, go with him twain. Give to him that asketh thee, and from him that would borrow of thee turn not thou away. Ye have heard that it hath been said, Thou shalt love thy neighbour, and hate thine enemy. But I say unto you, Love your enemies, bless them that curse you, do good to them that hate you, and pray for them which despitefully use you, and persecute you.
>
> MATTHEW 5:38-44

Jesus taught us that we should not only cease from resisting people who attack or take advantage of us, but that we should love those same people and treat them accordingly. If we are to be followers of Christ, we must obey His commandments. "For this is the love of God, that we keep his commandments: and his commandments are not grievous" (1 John 5:3). If we love God, we will keep His commandments, and they will not cause us grief.

In this passage from Matthew, Jesus gives us some real life examples of how to put this into action. Today, people are still attacked verbally, legally, materially, and even physically. If we resist, we are in opposition to our attacker. Jesus said that we should not resist evil. We must trust God to take care of us if we follow His commandments.

Variance

The Greek word *eris* is translated into English as "variance," and it means a quarrel. According to Webster, "quarrel" means to find fault, to disagree, to contend or dispute actively. Variance is actively opposing someone.

Variance is to argue with someone or something. Paul instructed Timothy that the man of God must not strive, meaning to war, quarrel, or dispute with. If people are open to hear and learn, speaking the truth in love may benefit them. If they are argumentative, it does no good to speak the truth to them. John 17:20–21 states: "Neither pray I for these alone, but for them also which shall believe on me through their word; That they may be one; as thou, Father, art in me, and I in thee, that they also may be one in us: that the world may believe that thou hast sent me."

What does it mean to be one? It means to be in total agreement, just as it was Paul's desire for the Corinthian church, as stated in 1 Corinthians 1:10: "Now I beseech you, brethren, by the name of our Lord Jesus Christ, that ye all speak the same thing, and that there be no divisions among you; but that ye be perfectly joined together in the same mind and in the same judgment."

To be one is to think the same way, understand things the same way, and speak the same things. This was the most earnest prayer of Jesus for His disciples and all of those who came to believe through their witness. This includes everyone who ever has or ever will come to believe in Jesus. This was also Paul's most earnest prayer for the Church. This is such an important issue that Paul identified it in his letter to the Ephesians as the first purpose of every ministry office.

> And he gave some, apostles; and some, prophets; and some, evangelists; and some, pastors and teachers; For the perfecting of the saints, for the work of the ministry, for the edifying of the body of Christ: Till we all come in the unity of the faith, and of the knowledge of the Son of God, unto a perfect man, unto the measure of the stature of the fullness of Christ: That we henceforth be no more children, tossed to and fro, and carried about with every wind of doctrine, by the sleight of men, and cunning craftiness, whereby they lie in wait to deceive; But speaking the truth in love, may grow up into him in all things, which is the head, even Christ.
>
> EPHESIANS 4:11-15

In verse 13, "Till we all come in the unity of the faith," means until we are without divisions. But how can we not have divisions? He goes on to explain.

When we all see Jesus the same way, understand His teachings the same way, and apply them to our lives in the same way, we will be the people whom God ordained us to be as followers of Christ. "Be ye therefore perfect, even as your Father which is in heaven is perfect" (Matthew 5:48). How perfect is the Father?

Jesus instructed that we should be as perfect as the Father, and He ordained all of the ministry offices to bring us to that point.

Most people think that this is totally impossible. They think it is ludicrous to even say such a thing. His definition of "perfect" is to love your enemies. "He maketh his sun to rise on the evil and on the good, and sendeth rain on the just and on the unjust" (Matthew 5:45). "Love your enemies, bless them that curse you, do good to them that hate you, and pray for them which despitefully use you, and persecute you" (Matthew 5:44). This is Jesus' definition of "perfect."

The purpose of the ministry is to bring us all to the place where this is how we live. This will only happen when we all grow up to be truly like Jesus in the way we think, speak, and act. Variance and divisions will not be eliminated by us simply accepting our differences. Our differences must be eliminated by "speaking the truth in love..." (Ephesians 4:15). Then judgment and persecution will make the Church spotless and without wrinkle.

Peter says, "For the time is come that judgment must begin at the house of God..." (1 Peter 4:17). Judgment brings persecution to drive out everything that is not like God. Judgment against the house of God has been going on from the time of Ananias and Sapphira, who fell dead for lying to the Holy Spirit (Acts 5:1–11). The reason this happened this way is found in Acts 2:46: "And they, continuing daily with one accord in the temple, and breaking bread from house to house, did eat their meat with gladness and singleness of heart."

There were no divisions among them, because they were "with one accord" and "singleness of heart." They were on the same page. They thought the same, they said the same things, and they did the same for the same purpose. There is great power when people are united.

Genesis 11:6 states: "And the Lord said, Behold, the people is one, and they have all one language; and this they begin to do: and now nothing will be restrained from them, which they have imagined to do."

God said that because they were one and had the same motivation, purpose, and goals, they could accomplish anything that they could imagine. Inventions come because someone begins to imagine and say, "What if we could do this or that?" Sometimes other people begin to get the vision and join in to help make it happen. If they do not succeed, someone in another place or generation takes up the torch and may use what the others learned to get a step ahead. Eventually someone will make it happen if they and others get the vision and continue. Research for cures for diseases happens this way. The key is to have a group of people who are one. God said that He would work to make His Church one. Those who claim to be God's people but do not live their lives in accordance with the teachings of Jesus will be subjected to correction from the Word of God. They will be corrected by men of God, and if they will not hear those, the world, the devil and his forces, and other tools at God's disposal will be used against them.

Paul instructed the Corinthian church to deal with one of its members because of his sin.

> For I verily, as absent in the body, but present in spirit, have judged already, as though I were present, concerning him that hath so done this deed, In the name of our Lord Jesus Christ, when ye are gathered together, and my spirit, with the power of our Lord Jesus Christ, To deliver such an one unto Satan for the destruction of the flesh, that the spirit may be saved in the day of the Lord Jesus.
>
> I CORINTHIANS 5:3-5

Paul instructed the Corinthian church to deliver this member to Satan for the destruction of the works of the flesh in his life, so that his spirit might be saved when Jesus returns. Satan is a tool to be used by God and the Church to eliminate the works of the flesh in the Church.

Our ministry is to warn the Church that God is going to work to purify His Church by using the powers of this world that are under Satan's control to bring fire on His Church to burn out the dross (impurities). This fire is being turned up more and more each day. The Bible declares that the Lord whom you seek shall sit as a refiner and purifier of silver, and that He shall purge the sons of Levi like silver and gold are purified. This is to make it possible for them to bring an offering to God in righteousness (Malachi 3:3).

When we turn to God and repent or change our ways, we are purified by the blood of Jesus. The fire compels us to give our lives totally to Him and to be governed by His teachings. The fire exists to drive the works of the flesh out of our lives. Have you given your life totally to Jesus? You can repent and give Him your life right now.

Emulations

The Greek word *zelos* is translated into English as "emulations." The English word "zeal" comes from this word. In a positive sense it means zeal, but in a negative sense it means jealousy.

Webster says that to be "jealous" is to be: intolerant of rivalry or unfaithfulness, disposed to suspect rivalry or unfaithfulness, apprehensive of the loss of another's exclusive devotion, hostile toward a rival or one believed to enjoy an advantage, vigilant in guarding a possession, distrustfully watchful, and suspicious.

Webster also defines "emulation" as ambitious or envious rivalry, so this is really about competitive pride. It is the desire to be equal or better than someone.

In Galatians 6:4 Paul instructs us this way: "But let every man prove his own work, and then shall he have rejoicing in himself alone, and not in another." The *New International Version* of the Bible states it this way: "Each one should test his own actions. Then he can take pride in himself, without comparing himself to somebody else." We should not put ourselves in a jealous competition with others. We are to check ourselves, without comparing ourselves to others.

Most people today do everything in a very selfish way. They drive aggressively, they fight over items when shopping, they cut in line anywhere they might have to wait, and generally act in a completely selfish way in public. This is a picture of emulation in action. Resist an evil, self-indulging person.

Wrath

The Greek word *thumos* is translated into English as "wrath." It means passion (as if breathing hard). It is to be so angry that one huffs and puffs and, if possible, he will blow your house down! Wrathful people are extremely angry.

James 1:19–20 states: "Wherefore, my beloved brethren, let every man be swift to hear, slow to speak, slow to wrath: For the wrath of man worketh not the righteousness of God."

In other words, when we get boiling mad, we are not likely to do those things that are pleasing to God. If we are swift to hear and slow to speak, we will probably be slow to wrath. When you feel angry, keep your mouth shut and listen. Then choose to forgive as an act of your will. Dead people do not hold anger or grudges in their heart. If we are dead to sin, we can live for Christ and hold no animosity toward others in our heart.

Strife

The Greek word *eritheia* is translated into English as "strife." It means intrigue and, by implication, faction. Webster defines "faction" as a selfish or contentious group. To "strive" is defined as having to struggle in opposition or contend. This really means to struggle or to take sides. It often takes the form of a verbal disagreement.

Paul wrote in 2 Timothy 2:24, "And the servant of the Lord must not strive; but be gentle unto all men, apt to teach, patient." It accomplishes nothing just to argue with people. If people do not receive you, Jesus gave very specific instructions on how to deal with such a situation.

Luke 9:5 states: "And whosoever will not receive you, when ye go out of that city, shake off the very dust from your feet for a testimony against them."

If people do not receive our message, we are to leave them and shake the dust of their place off of us for a testimony against them, but we are not to stay and argue with them. Paul also said that we should avoid foolish and unlearned questions, because they produce strife (2 Timothy 2:23).

Seditions

The Greek word *dichostasia* is translated into English as "seditions." It means disunion and, figuratively, dissension. Webster defines "sedition" as incitement of resistance to, or insurrection against, lawful authority. Webster adds this comment, "Treason means a serious breach of allegiance. Sedition implies conduct leading to or inciting commotion or resistance to authority, but without overt acts of violence or betrayal."

One form of sedition is nonviolent protest. It is being in resistance to authority without overt acts of violence or betrayal. This is not consistent with the fruit or what the Spirit of God produces in our lives.

> Let every soul be subject unto the higher powers. For there is no power but of God: the powers that be are ordained of God. Whosoever therefore resisteth the power, resisteth the ordinance of God: and they that resist shall receive to themselves damnation. For rulers are not a terror to good works, but to the evil. Wilt thou then not be afraid of the power? do that which is good, and thou shalt have praise of the same.
>
> ROMANS 13:1-3

Paul emphatically states that there is no government that is not ordained of God. This can appear to be hard to believe. Governments that attack their own people for political reasons do not look to be what God would put in power, but throughout history God has had a purpose for everyone that He has put in power. Most of the time, He has given the people the leaders for whom they asked, just as the children of Israel asked Samuel for a king.

Samuel told them that they did not need a king, but God told Samuel to anoint Saul as their king, because they rejected God as their leader. Most governments come to power because the people want them in power. After they are in power, the people may no longer want them, but they did at one point in time.

Saul wanted to kill David, even though David had done nothing bad to him. Saul threw a spear at him and pursued him with an army, trying to kill him for no good reason. David refused to raise his hand against Saul, because David knew Saul was God's anointed. David had opportunities to kill Saul, but he refused to kill him.

Saul was wounded in battle. He fell on a sword, but he was still alive. When a young Amalekite was passing by, Saul asked him to kill him so that the Philistines would not find him still alive. The young man killed him just as he asked. The young man brought Saul's crown and bracelet to David and told him what had happened. The young man told David that he was sure Saul was going to die, so he killed Saul in response to his request.

"And David said unto him, How was thou not afraid to stretch forth thine hand to destroy the Lord's anointed? And David called one of the young men, and said, Go near, and fall upon him. And he smote him that he died" (2 Samuel 1:14–15). The man who came and told David that his enemy Saul was dead was executed at David's order. In David's mind, Saul was still God's anointed, even when Saul was trying to kill David for no reason. This was the respect that David showed for the leader that God had placed over the nation, even when he was a total reprobate. He did not stop showing respect even when Saul was trying to kill him for no reason.

Remember, Paul said there is no leadership that is not ordained by God. We must be subject to the powers that be. This includes those in positions of authority, such as parents, leadership in school, at work, in all levels of government, in law enforcement, in church, and in every other institution ordained by God.

Heresies

Vines Expository Dictionary of Biblical Words says that the Greek word for "heresies" is *hairesis,* which denotes a choosing or a choice (from *haireomai* "to choose"). It is that which is chosen, and hence, an opinion, especially a self-willed opinion, which is substituted for submission to the power of the truth, and leads to division and the formation of sects, Gal. 5:20 (marg., "parties"); such erroneous opinions are frequently the outcome of personal preference or the prospect of advantage. See 2 Peter 2:1 where "destructive" signifies leading to ruin.

Heresies are simply opinions that are not based on the truth. Second Timothy 2:15 says, "Study to shew thyself approved unto God, a workman that needeth not to be ashamed, rightly dividing the word of truth." In other words, study so God will approve of you, because you interpret God's Word correctly. Then you do not have to be ashamed, because you failed to teach God's Word correctly.

On judgment day we do not want to find ourselves among those who were ever studying, but never able to come to the knowledge of the truth. We do not wish to find ourselves among those who would not endure sound doctrine, but gathered to ourselves teachers who taught us things that we wanted to hear to satisfy our own desires (2 Timothy 3:7, 4:3).

Doctrine cannot be based upon our opinions or experiences, unless they are consistent with the Word of God. Our experiences must be interpreted in light of God's Word and not the other way around. Therefore, we do not even have the ability to understand our own experiences unless we have a good understanding of His Word.

Most people are taught doctrine before they learn God's Word. The problem is that they interpret God's Word in light of their doctrine rather than forming their doctrine from God's Word. Many people in this situation cannot be helped.

Matthew 9:16–17 states: "No man putteth a piece of new

cloth unto an old garment, for that which is put in to fill it up taketh from the garment, and the rent is made worse. Neither do men put new wine into old bottles: else the bottles break, and the wine runneth out, and the bottles perish: but they put new wine into new bottles, and both are preserved."

In this parable, Jesus teaches that we cannot patch a person's doctrine or empty his doctrine out and fill him with new doctrine. In another place, He stated that no one having drunk old wine and then new says that the new is better, but he thinks the old is better. This means that when we bring new doctrine to a person who is full of another or old doctrine, he does not accept the new as being better. If he is full of bad doctrine, he may be in trouble.

When someone hears doctrine that is different from what he already believes, he chooses to either truly consider the new doctrine or to reject it because it does not fit with what he believes.

> And the brethren immediately sent away Paul and Silas by night unto Berea: who coming thither went into the synagogue of the Jews. These were more noble than those in Thessalonica, in that they received the word with all readiness of mind, and searched the scriptures daily, whether those things were so. Therefore many of them believed; also of honourable women which were Greeks, and of men, not a few.
>
> ACTS 17:10-12

What made these people more honorable was that they received the Word with an open mind and searched the scriptures daily to see if this new doctrine was backed by the scriptures. They did not judge them based on the doctrines that they had already been taught, but against God's Word. The result was that many of them believed.

We must realize that believing in something does not necessarily make it true. It simply means that we have perceived it to be true. Whether or not it is true can only be judged against a standard.

All of the Protestant reformers held that the Bible would be the sole basis for doctrine. We believe that fulfilled prophecies and present-day miracles validate the Bible, just as Mark 16:20 says: "And they went forth, and preached every where, the Lord working with them, and confirming the word with signs following." God has always confirmed His Word with miracles.

Moses saw a bush that was on fire but not burning up, and the bush talked to him. Some people put out a fleece to find God's will. Jesus told the disciples to believe the miracles that He did, even if they did not believe what He said. Today is no different. God still confirms His Word with miracles. We must receive the truth.

Hosea 4:6 states: "My people are destroyed for lack of knowledge: because thou has rejected knowledge, I will also reject thee, that thou shalt be no priest to me: seeing thou hast forgotten the law of thy God, I will also forget thy children."

God said that His people—not some other people—are destroyed for lack of knowledge. This is because they reject the knowledge of the truth that comes from God's law. Any people who reject knowledge that comes from God's law are in deep trouble. They reject God's law by not keeping it.

Romans 2:13 says, "For not the hearers of the law are just before God, but the doers of the law shall be justified." As you discover the truth of God's law, put it into practice in your life or it will profit you nothing.

The Bible says that all scripture originates with God and is good to teach us what to believe, to tell us when we are wrong, and to tell us how to be in a right relationship with God. This is so that the man of God may be all that he is supposed to be, and do all that he is supposed to do (2 Timothy 3:16–17). Base your doctrine on the Word of God after very careful study.

Envyings

The Greek word *phthonos* is translated into English as "envyings," which means ill-will (as detraction). Webster defines "detraction" as a lessening of reputation or esteem, especially by envious, malicious, or petty criticism. Webster defines "envy" as malice, painful or resentful awareness of an advantage enjoyed by another joined with a desire to possess the same advantage.

In Bible terminology, this is covetousness or lust. In another place, Paul identifies people who will enter the kingdom of God!

First Corinthians 6:9–10 states: "Know ye not that the unrighteous shall not inherit the kingdom of God? Be not deceived: neither fornicators, nor idolaters, nor adulterers, nor effeminate, nor abusers of themselves with mankind, Nor thieves, nor <u>covetous</u>, nor drunkards, nor revilers, nor extortioners, shall inherit the kingdom of God."

People who do these things will not be in heaven! Paul asks if we do not know this. Then he tells us not to be fooled. I ask the same question: Don't you know that people who do these things will not be in heaven?

Webster defines "covet" as to wish for enviously. When we wish for something enviously, we covet. Hebrews 13:5 says, "Let your conversation be without covetousness; and be content with such things as ye have: for he hath said, I will never leave thee, nor forsake thee."

The writer of Hebrews said that we should be happy with what we have, because the Lord said that He would always be with us to take care of our needs. He goes on to say that we can say that we will not fear what people may do to us, because the Lord is our helper (Hebrews 13:6).

In the world today we are constantly bombarded with commercials that are designed to produce covetousness in our hearts. They tell us about all of the things that we need. Much of the fashion industry is open about the fact that they want to dress people in a way that will produce lust in the hearts of others. These things are designed to produce covetousness in your heart that will ensure that you will spend eternity in hell. We should be content with the things that we already have. If we seek the kingdom of God, He will supply all that we need.

Murders

The Greek word *phonos* is translated into English as "murders," and it means to slay. "Murder" means the same thing in Greek that it does in English. It means to kill. You are probably thinking that you would never do anything like that.

> Ye have heard that it was said by them of old time, Thou shalt not kill; and whosoever shall kill shall be in danger of the judgment: But I say unto you, That whosoever is angry with his brother without a cause shall be in danger of the judgment: and whosoever shall say to his brother, Raca, shall be in danger of the council: but whosoever shall say, Thou fool, shall be in danger of hell fire.
>
> MATTHEW 5:21-22

"Raca" is an Aramaic term that probably should be translated "empty head." Aramaic is the Assyrian language, and it came in Israel when the Assyrians conquered the northern kingdom of Israel during the divided kingdom period.

Jesus said that if we call another person a fool, we are in danger of spending eternity in hell. In other words, to call someone a fool is on the same level as committing murder in our thinking.

> And the tongue is a fire, a world of iniquity: so is the tongue among our members, that it defileth the whole body, and setteth on fire the course of nature; and it is set on fire of hell...But the tongue can no man tame; it is an unruly evil, full of deadly poison. Therewith bless we God, even the Father; and therewith curse we men, which are made after the similitude of God.
>
> JAMES 3:6, 8-9

James says that with the same tongue we bless God and curse men, who are made in the image of God. This cannot be. We must rule over our tongue. We must leave the placement of curses to God. Hebrews 10:30 says, "For we know him that hath said, Vengeance belongeth unto me, I will recompense, saith the Lord. And again, The Lord shall judge his people." The Lord is the one whose job it is to judge people and give them what they have coming, whether good or bad. It is not our job!

Matthew 7:1–2 states: "Judge not, that ye be not judged. For with what judgment ye judge, ye shall be judged: and with what measure ye mete, it shall be measured to you again."

We should not judge other people because only God knows the thoughts and intents of the hearts of men. If we judge others without knowing all of the facts, which are impossible for us to know, we will be judged without all of the facts being considered. This would not be a good thing for you and me. Do not judge, criticize, and condemn other people. Just speak the truth in love to those who will listen.

Drunkenness

The Greek word *methe* is translated into English as "drunkenness," and it means an intoxicant or to be intoxicated. While the Bible does not prohibit drinking alcoholic beverages, it teaches strongly against the people of God becoming intoxicated or drunk.

Ephesians 5:18 says, "And be not drunk with wine, wherein is excess; but be filled with the Spirit." Alcohol generally loosens our inhibitions, which is something on the inside of us that works to control our carnal nature.

This chapter is about not allowing your carnal nature to control your actions, thoughts, or attitudes. Why would we fill up on something that is going to work to prevent us from reaching our goal?

Many people are killed by drunk drivers every year. Many violent crimes are committed by people who are under the influence of alcohol. Not everyone who has a drink kills someone or commits a violent crime, but many who kill or commit violent crimes have been drinking. Be filled with the Spirit.

Alcoholic beverages are called "spirits," and they are a cheap imitation of the feelings that a person can experience from close encounters with the Holy Spirit. Peter says that believing in Jesus produces "joy unspeakable" (1 Peter 1:8). That is joy that is too great to be described with words. You may have gone to church all of your life and never experienced anything like that. If so, you have been missing something, because that joy is available from the Holy Spirit. Seek the Lord while He may be found, and you will find "joy unspeakable."

Revellings

The Greek word *komos* is translated into English as "revellings," and it means a carousal (as if letting loose). This is letting your hair down or letting go of your inhibitions. "It's the weekend, so let's party and forget our troubles. Have some fun! Kick up our heels! Let's boogie!"

These are all expressions that deal with this idea. We can have a good time without letting go of our inhibitions or getting out of control. There's nothing wrong with having a good time, but there's plenty wrong with getting out of control.

Paul said, "If after the manner of men I have fought with beasts at Ephesus, what advantageth it me, if the dead rise not? let us eat and drink; for tomorrow we die" (1 Corinthians 15:32). In other words, what good did it do me to endure being put in the arena in Ephesus to fight for my life with wild animals because of my Christian witness if there is no resurrection from the dead? We should eat, drink, and be merry before we die if there is no life after death. In another place, he said that we are to be pitied above all men if we live to secure the next life and there is no next life.

Romans 8:24 says, "For we are saved by hope: but hope that is seen is not hope: for what a man seeth, why doth he yet hope for?" We are saved, believing that there is a life after death, but it is a matter of faith to believe. If we could see it, we would not have to hope that it exists. We make the choice to believe. By faith, we live for another life in another place that we cannot see.

If this is true, we must set our affection on things above, not on, things on the earth (Colossians 3:2). If you do not have that "peace that passes understanding" and "joy unspeakable," give your life totally to Jesus and learn to trust Him completely. Then you will find these things.

If you have any of these "vital signs" in your life, repent and seek the Lord with all of your heart so that your spirit may be saved in the day of our Lord. Give your life totally to the Lord. He is able to make out of you what He wants you to be. It is not up to you. He will transform you as you follow His commandments.

CHAPTER SIX

FAITH: THE POWER TO SUCCEED

WE HAVE DISCUSSED how to become a disciple of Jesus, things that cause the Word of God to not produce fruit in people's lives, and "vital signs" that show that God's Word has not produced the desired fruit in people's lives. Now we will discuss the ingredient that must be added to the Word of God to produce the proper results.

Hebrews 4:2 states: "For unto us was the gospel preached, as well as unto them: but the word preached did not profit them, not being mixed with faith in them that heard it."

Faith is the ingredient that must be mixed with the Word of God for it to produce the intended results in our lives. If we do not absolutely believe the Word of God, it will not work for us.

"Now faith is the substance of things hoped for, the evidence of things not seen" (Hebrews 11:1). Faith is what makes the things for which we hope real to us. It is what made Abraham believe that he could have a son by his wife Sarah when he was about one hundred years old and she was about ninety. Faith is what gave him the ability to take Isaac to Mount Moriah to offer him as a sacrifice to God at His command. Abraham believed that even if God had to raise Isaac from the ashes after he killed and burned him as a sacrifice to God, he would have descendants through Isaac. Faith that God would do what He said, in spite of anything that might happen, is what gave him the ability to obey.

Faith is believing in the existence of what cannot be seen, felt, heard, smelled, or tasted. Faith in God bases its confidence in the unerring magnitude of God. How big is God?

Satan was face-to-face with God for who knows how long. One day he decided that he could beat God, and one-third of the angels believed it too. He was the most powerful thing that God made (Ezekiel 28:11–19). Jesus told us how long the fight lasted. "He said unto them, I beheld Satan as lightning fall from heaven" (Luke 10:18).

When the most powerful being in creation stood up to God, he lasted a split second. Anything that stands up to you is not much of a challenge for God. This is why Romans 8:31 declares, "If God be for us, who can be against us?" Faith in God is being totally confident of God's power and love.

When I am totally confident that God is for me, because I know that He loves me, I can believe that the Lord will provide all that I need and do everything that I ask that is in line with His will. Faith is being totally confident of God's love, and God is love.

Hebrews 11:5–6 states: "By faith Enoch was translated that he should not see death; and was not found, because God had translated him: for before his translation he had this testimony, that he pleased God. But without faith it is impossible to please him; for he that cometh to God must believe that he is, and that he is a rewarder of them that diligently seek him."

Enoch had this testimony that he pleased God. When your life is pleasing to God, you know that He is for you. But it is impossible for your life to be pleasing to God unless you trust Him.

Faith is believing that God exists and that He rewards those who diligently seek Him. What does it mean to reward? A reward is something to be desired. God gives good and desirable things to those who constantly seek Him. If we do not believe this, it is impossible to please God. But all that we really need to know is that God is for us.

Romans 8:31–33 states: "What shall we then say to these things? If God be for us, who can be against us? He that spared not his own Son, but delivered him up for us all, how shall he not with him also freely give us all things? Who shall lay any thing to the charge of God's elect? It is God that justifieth."

God is for us. He sent His Son so that we could be given a right relationship with Him. Jesus died for us, and He is not going to point His finger at those who give their lives to Him. Does this mean that we will not be judged for the things we do that are not according to God's will? It most certainly does not! It simply means that God is for us, not against us.

Romans 6:15–16 states: "What then? shall we sin, because we are not under the law, but under grace? God forbid. Know ye not, that to whom ye yield yourselves servants to obey, his servants ye are to whom ye obey; whether of sin unto death, or of obedience unto righteousness?"

Whoever you choose to obey—Jesus' commands or temptation from your natural desires—will determine to whom you belong: Jesus or your flesh. Are your natural desires (flesh) in control of your life or is Jesus? If your flesh controls you, you will spend eternity in hell. What gives you the ability to yield to God is faith in God. You can only obey those whom you trust.

Faith may start as a matter of choice. We choose to believe that God exists and that He will take care of us if we live for Him. We choose to trust that He is willing and able to keep that which we have committed to Him against that day, or we trust that He is willing and able do what is necessary to make sure that we receive a good report on judgment day.

As we begin to live the Christian life, we begin to really know the Lord if we spend enough quality time with Him—reading, studying, and meditating on His words and talking to Him (praying) at length on a regular basis. After all, what does it take to develop a close relationship with anyone? It takes spending a lot of quality, intimate time with a person to really build a trusting relationship with him or her. It takes the same things to build a close relationship with Almighty God.

The Lord began to reveal Himself to people a long time ago. These events are recorded in the Bible. He began to reveal Himself to Moses many years ago, and He told Moses that He was the "I AM." In other words, "I am the God who exists." Then He was called "the Living God." This is because the other gods were made of wood, stone, gold, or some other natural material. Other societies had imaginary gods like Zeus, Athena, Diana, or many others too numerous to list. But the great "I AM" is the only living God.

Of all the miraculous stories in the Old Testament, the exodus from Egypt is one of the most famous. A central theme throughout all of scripture is displaying the unmatched power of Almighty God. Paul says in Romans, chapter 1, that all of creation testifies to God's existence and power. The exodus experience is a demonstration of a little of God's power and His willingness to use it for the benefit of His people.

Exodus 9:16 states: "And in very deed for this cause have I raised thee up, for to shew in thee my power; and that my name may be declared throughout all the earth."

This statement is addressed to the Pharaoh of Egypt. God made Pharaoh the most powerful man on the face of the earth through the hand of the man Joseph so that he could show that the most powerful man on earth was no problem for God to handle. From the beginning of the story, the Bible states that God hardened Pharaoh's heart. Pharaoh did not harden his heart, but God did so that He could bring another plague on the Egyptians to demonstrate more of His power and willingness to use it for the benefit of His people. God is willing to do whatever is required to set you free from whatever has you bound. Whether it is an addiction, greed, sickness, or any other thing, God can and will set you free.

He sent His son to set us free from the works of the devil. Sin, sickness, and poverty are just a few of those things. The Bible says that Jesus became poor so that we might be rich. But remember, Jesus said that if we cannot be trusted with "unrighteous mammon" (money and material things), who would trust us with true riches?

True riches are faith, hope, love, and the power of God. Peter declared that faith is more valuable than silver and gold. Faith enables you to have God's power at your disposal, but money will only get for you what people can do. God has immensely more power and ability than people. Real faith makes God's power available to those who believe.

Jesus demonstrated some of the things that could be accomplished by people who have God's power available to them. He healed the sick, miraculously escaped from people who were trying to kill Him in His hometown, walked on water, and did many other things that are truly amazing. He stated that those who believe would do greater works than He did.

John 14:12–14 states: "Verily, verily, I say unto you, He that believeth on me, the works that I do shall he do also; and greater works than these shall he do; because I go unto my Father. And whatsoever ye shall ask in my name, that will I do, that the Father may be glorified in the Son. If ye ask any thing in my name, I will do it."

Jesus Himself stated that those who believe shall do greater works than He did, and He will do anything that we ask. The only condition is to believe. If we have faith as big as a mustard seed, which is very small, we can say to a mountain to be uprooted and planted in the ocean and it will obey us! Either we have faith or we do not! The proof is in the pudding!

No job is too big or too small. Paul said that if we speak with the tongues of men and angels, or in their language and have not love, then it is of no value. If we have faith that can move mountains and understand all mysteries, but have not love, it is of no value. This says that the motivation behind the operation of faith, tongues, and knowledge must be love. The greatest quality of all is love for God and for people.

All of these things come from the knowledge of God's Word. It is the knowledge of God's love revealed in the scriptures that produces faith in our hearts and hope for eternal life. True riches are the revelation of God's love in our hearts. We can know the words printed in the Bible, yet not know the love of God. It must be revealed to our hearts by the Holy Spirit. Then faith comes in our hearts.

In studying faith, I found first of all that faith comes by hearing, and hearing comes by the Word of God (Romans 10:17).

When Jesus would teach, He finished many times by saying, "He that hath ears to hear, let him hear." The letters to the churches in Revelation all end with Jesus saying, "He that hath an ear, let him hear what the Spirit saith unto the churches" (Revelation 2:7, 11, 17, 29; 3:6, 13, 22).

Obviously, He was not referring to the physical ears on our heads. Everyone had those. He was referring to spiritual ears. The Spirit of God does not normally speak audibly to people, although there are exceptions to this. Jesus said that God is a spirit. He normally speaks in the spiritual realm. Those who are spiritually sensitive can hear Him and recognize His voice. Jesus said, "My sheep hear my voice, and I know them, and they follow me" (John 10:27). Just because we hear the words that are in the Bible does not mean that we hear what God is saying.

> Wherefore I also, after I heard of your faith in the Lord Jesus, and love unto all the saints, Cease not to give thanks for you, making mention of you in my prayers; That the God of our Lord Jesus Christ, the Father of glory, may give unto you the spirit of wisdom and revelation in the knowledge of him: The eyes of your understanding being enlightened; that ye may know what is the hope of his calling, and what the riches of the glory of his inheritance in the saints.
> EPHESIANS 1:15–18

Paul prayed that God would give these people the "spirit of wisdom and revelation." People do not naturally have the ability to understand God's message. Unless He gives us the spirit of wisdom and revelation, we cannot "see the forest for the trees."

One day, Jesus fed about five thousand men, besides women and children, with five loaves of bread and two fish (Matthew 14:21). Later, He fed four thousand men, besides women and children, with seven loaves and a few little fishes (Matthew 15:38). After they crossed the Sea of Galilee, He told the disciples to "beware of the leaven of the Pharisees and of the Sadducees" (Matthew 16:6). The disciples thought He said this because they had forgotten to bring bread with them.

Jesus then asked the disciples if they had already forgotten about the five loaves and the five thousand, or the seven loaves and the four thousand, or how much they had left over.

Matthew 16:11–12 states: "How is it that ye do not understand that I spake it not to you concerning bread, that ye should beware of the leaven of the Pharisees and of the Sadducees? Then understood they how he bade them not beware of the leaven of bread, but of the doctrine of the Pharisees and of the Sadducees."

When Jesus made a spiritual statement about being wary of the "leaven" or doctrines of the Pharisees and Sadducees, the disciples had no understanding of what He was saying. He had to explain it to them. They did not have the spiritual ability to understand what He was saying.

First Corinthians 2:13–14 states: "Which things also we speak, not in the words which man's wisdom teacheth, but which the Holy Ghost teacheth; comparing spiritual things with spiritual. But the natural man receiveth not the things of the Spirit of God: for they are foolishness unto him: neither can he know them, because they are spiritually discerned."

People who do not have the Holy Spirit to give them the spirit of wisdom and understanding have no ability to understand spiritual words. Therefore, they cannot hear them, because they are spiritually discerned or understood. This is why Jesus said that those who have ears should hear what the Spirit is saying.

It follows, then, that "faith cometh by hearing, and hearing by the word of God" (Romans 10:17). People who are not spiritually discerning cannot have real faith. They can hear the words, but they cannot truly hear the message.

I noticed also that faith is listed among the "fruit of the Spirit" (Galatians 5:22), and among the "gifts" or manifestations of the Spirit (1 Corinthians 12:9). In both instances, faith is produced by the Spirit of God in a person's heart. It is faith from the Spirit of God that is produced in a person's heart. The Spirit of God gives us the ability to hear or understand the message, and the Spirit of God then produces faith in our hearts.

The closer relationship we develop with the Holy Spirit, the more faith we will have in God. Faith is really the product of a relationship.

Sin is the transgression of God's law (1 John 3:4). Living in sin and disobedience causes the hearts of people to become hard. Those who are in regular contact with the law, and yet do not obey it, are the most hard-hearted of all. These are mainly religious people.

Second Corinthians 11:13–15 (NIV) states: "For such men are false apostles, deceitful workmen, masquerading as apostles of Christ. And no wonder, for Satan himself masquerades as an angel of light. It is not surprising, then, if his servants are masquerading as servants of righteousness. Their end will be what their actions deserve."

This says that some preachers are Satan's main workers. I could not understand this for a long time. People are often puzzled why Jesus could spend much of His time with prostitutes, sinners, and tax collectors, and not with the religious people of His day. He spoke very kindly to the sinners, but very harshly to the false religious leaders.

In war, if a man pretends to be on one side but is really working for the other side, he is a spy. Prisoners of war are protected by the Geneva Convention, but spies are shot.

A preacher who opposes the work of God is, in reality, a double agent, whether he realizes it or not. He does not really perceive that he is opposing the work of God, just as Saul of Tarsus did not perceive that he was trying to destroy the Church of God. That does not change the fact that those who listen to him and believe him are led astray by his words and actions. He does the most harm to God's work.

It was not prostitutes, bar owners, thieves, or other sinners who were rounding up all of the Christians and killing or imprisoning them. Only this man with a great zeal for God, but not according to knowledge, was doing that. He perceived himself to be doing God a great service when, in fact, he was God's greatest enemy. In Saul's case, however, God turned that great zeal around by showing him the error of his ways.

Not all preachers are enemies of God. Jesus said that we can recognize them by examining what they say and do in the light of God's Word. Paul told the people to be steadfast in the gospel that he had preached to them, and to follow his example in living. Some preachers are men of God, and some are enemies of God. We can tell the difference by comparing them to Jesus. If they show the same spirit, speak the same words, and do the same things, they are men of God.

Those who are men of God will have faith like Jesus and they will be moved with compassion like Jesus. This compassion will cause them to preach the gospel, feed the hungry, clothe the naked, heal the sick, and set the captives free (Luke 4:18–19). This faith controls what we think, say, and do. I began to experience this in my life the day that I really met Jesus.

I gave my life totally to Jesus at thirty-five years of age. After midnight that day, I was on my knees beside my bed talking to God. I have two daughters who have asthma. When they begin to cough in their sleep, it means that an asthma attack is starting. As I was talking to God, I heard one of them begin to cough. I said, "God, I don't have time to mess with that now because I am talking to you. Would you take care of that?" I was not well-trained and versed in healing and faith. I had very little contact with healing and no teaching in faith prior to that moment. The coughing stopped as quickly as turning off a light.

In a few moments, however, I heard the coughing start up again. I stopped praying and stood up. The only way that I can describe the feeling that I had is one of total unbelief. I could not believe that I was hearing coughing again. I said to God in an angry tone of voice, "God, I asked you to take care of that!"

I walked down the hall to the room where my daughter who was coughing the first time was sleeping. Then I heard the cough behind me! It was not the same girl coughing! The first was my oldest daughter, but the second was my youngest. Suddenly, I realized that I was wrong. I apologized to the Lord and asked Him to take care of that one also. It stopped as quickly as turning off a light.

I prayed approximately two more hours before going to bed. The rest of the night was undisturbed by asthma or any other attack of the devil.

I learned several things from this experience. At least two of them apply to what we are studying. First of all, I learned that faith is present in those who are in the Spirit to the degree that they are in the Spirit. As I said, this was the first time that I had been in church in years. I had not been reading the Bible. I had not been trained in healing or faith. I had some contact with healing previously, but not even enough to remember at that time.

Many times, people who have attended or even preached in Word of Faith Charismatic churches for years do not have these kinds of results. Some do, but not all. I believe in reading and studying for many reasons, including the renewing of the mind (Romans 12:2). As we have already shown, however, reading and studying the Word will not in itself produce faith without the Holy Spirit revealing the Word to the heart of the reader.

The second thing that I learned from this experience is how faith reacts to circumstances that make it appear that God has not responded to faith's request. This is a natural reaction from the heart, not a taught or "faith" action. It is not forced, but it is totally natural. To react any other way would take tremendous self-restraint. Real faith totally and completely expects to see the answer to the request or need. There is absolutely no doubt about it.

Jesus said that if we believe with our heart, not just with our mind, and not doubt, we will have the things that we say (Mark 11:23–24). In other words, whatever we say is going to happen according to God's will (1 John 5:14–15). Like when Elijah told Ahab that it would not rain until he said and it did not rain for three-and-a-half years. We can have the things that we say when we say God's will.

Faith speaks things that other people do not say. Faith does not speak what it sees in the physical world, but what it expects to be produced by the will and power of God. The Bible says that God calls things that be not as though they were (Romans 4:17).

Just as God spoke creation into existence, and said, "Let there be light," when there was no light, then there was light. These things were done by the power of His words. The power behind the words was the Holy Spirit, and circumstances moved in response to God's Word.

The Bible says that God created man in His image, after His likeness, and gave him dominion over everything in creation (Genesis 1:26). Man exercised his dominion with his voice. No other earthly creature was given the power to choose and speak its own words. The power is the Holy Spirit, and He responds to God's Word spoken in faith.

If we have given our lives totally to Jesus, we have a right, like a power of attorney, to use His name to direct the power of God (Mark 16:17, Luke 10:17). Evil spirits are subject to those who have a right to speak in the name of Jesus. Jesus has complete authority over heaven and earth now. Matthew 28:18 says, "And Jesus came and spake unto them, saying, All power is given unto me in heaven and in earth."

The Greek word *exousia* is translated in other places as authority, jurisdiction, liberty, right, power, and strength. He said that all authority and jurisdiction over heaven and earth are His now. This was not always true.

Luke 4:5–6 states: "And the devil, taking him up into an high mountain, shewed unto him all the kingdoms of the world in a moment of time. And the devil said unto him, All this power will I give thee, and the glory of them: for that is delivered unto me; and to whomsoever I will I give it."

At this point in time, that authority over the world systems of this earth belonged to the devil. When Jesus died for the sins of the whole world, the devil's authority over the earth was revoked and given to Jesus. The devil had gotten it from man by enticing him to sin in the garden, but Jesus took it back by taking away that sin.

Second Corinthians 5:21 says, "For he hath made him to be sin for us, who knew no sin; that we might be made the righteousness of God in him." The scapegoat to the Old Testament is the picture of Jesus taking our sin away. Whoever pays the price for anything receives ownership of that thing. Jesus paid the price for the authority over the earth.

God did not give the earth to man, only dominion over it. Therefore, the devil did not receive ownership of the world, only authority over it. Psalm 24:1 states, "The earth is the Lord's, and the fulness thereof…" Haggai 2:8 says, "The silver is mine, and the gold is mine, saith the Lord of hosts." Even the cattle on a thousand hills are the Lord's, according to Psalm 50:10. Now Jesus has dominion over it. Those who have given their lives totally to Him receive the right to use His authority in the earth, and everything on earth is subject to His authority.

The person who has given his life totally to Jesus and finds that this authority is available to him or her can exercise it. If they try to use it improperly, it will not work. This power must be carried out by the Holy Spirit, for He will not do things that are against the will of God. Since the authority belongs to Jesus and not to man, man cannot give it back to the devil again by sinning or in any other way.

Since we know that the Holy Spirit responds to our words that are spoken in faith in line with the will of God and the Word of God, we can have great faith if we know the will of God. The two things that inhibit our faith are not knowing the will of God and disobedience to Jesus' commands. If we live in disobedience, we become "outlaws" and lose our confidence to speak for and to the Lord until we repent and are forgiven.

John 15:6–7 states: "If a man abide not in me, he is cast forth as a branch, and is withered; and men gather them, and cast them into the fire, and they are burned. If ye abide in me, and my words abide in you, ye shall ask what ye will, and it shall be done unto you."

To be a Christian is to be "in Him." There are many opinions as to what is necessary to be a Christian, but the Bible is very specific. It tells us how to know if we are "in Him."

1 John 2:4–5 states: "He that saith, I know him, and keepeth not his commandments, is a liar, and the truth is not in him. But whoso keepeth his word, in him verily is the love of God perfected: hereby know we that we are in him."

If we keep His word, if we put His commandments into effect in our lives, we know that we are in Him. If we do not do the things that He said to do and still claim to know Him, we are liars and the truth is not in us.

1 John 5:18 states: "We know that whosoever is born of God sinneth not; but he that is begotten of God keepeth himself, and the wicked one toucheth him not."

This says that if you are born of God, you will not allow yourself to sin, but you will keep yourself so the devil cannot cause you to do wrong things. You may say, "This is not possible, because who do you know who does not sin?"

First of all, I am not going to allow my experience to negate the Word of God. My perception of my experience may be wrong. I know that God's Word is true, so I must understand my experience in light of God's Word and not understand God's Word in light of my experience. Jesus said that heaven and earth would pass away, but His Word would remain.

The key to understanding this is to know that our ability to live in accordance with God's Word is not dependent upon our strength, but upon God's strength and ability. God is able to keep His people blameless until the day of our Lord (1 Corinthians 1:8).

Jude 24 says, "Now unto him that is able to keep you from falling, and to present you faultless before the presence of his glory with exceeding joy."

It is God's ability that is in question, not ours. The Bible says that He has given us everything that pertains to life and godliness (2 Peter 1:3). He has given us everything that is needed to be godly. He has given us His Spirit, His Word, and men of God to instruct and empower us to live a holy, righteous life. We must approach this in a spirit of faith.

We must say, like Paul, that we have believed and therefore we have spoken (2 Corinthians 4:13). There is not anything we need that God has not provided. Live a holy and righteous life, abide in Him and let His Word abide in you so that you can accomplish this. It is absolutely necessary to know and keep His commandments to do this.

Bible study must become one of the most important things in your life. Prayer, praise, and worship to God must be more important to us than eating and sleeping. These things must supersede everything else in our lives. When they do, we will be strong in faith, giving glory to God and receiving the things that we say.

Many times God answers cries for help that are not spoken in faith because of His mercy. If the people were always strong in faith, they would speak to the problem, not cry out in fear or desperation. The products of faith are peace and joy, not fear and anxiety. But these prayers are not answered in response to faith. The answers come as a product of God's love, mercy, and grace.

In the twelfth chapter of Acts, we find the story of Peter's imprisonment by Herod the king. Verse five says, "Peter therefore was kept in prison: but prayer was made without ceasing of the church unto God for him." God sent an angel and delivered him from the prison in the middle of the night.

Peter was not expecting to be delivered because he did not believe it when it happened. He thought that he was seeing a vision or a dream (Acts 12:9). After he came to himself and thought about it, he went to the house of Mary, the mother of John Mark. There were many gathered there who had been praying all night, but they were not in faith. When he came to the door, the girl who answered it became so excited that she ran back to tell the people without letting Peter inside.

When she told them that Peter was at the door, they said, "Thou art mad…" (Acts 12:15). She said, "Oh, yes, it's really Peter," and they replied, "No, it's his angel (ghost)." But the "ghost" kept on knocking on the door. When they opened the door and saw him, they did not say, "We knew that you were coming because we have been praying to God for your release." They were amazed that he was really there.

Obviously, they were not praying in faith, believing that God was going to answer their prayer quickly or any other way. They were not thoroughly convinced in their heart that God would quickly answer their prayer—but God answered their prayer anyway! He is a God of love and mercy! We must grow in faith and learn to believe. We cannot please Him unless we believe (Hebrews 11:6).

One day when I picked up my Bible to read, the Lord told me to read 2 Samuel 17. I also felt impressed to read the last verse of the preceding chapter. After this happened a couple of days in a row, I decided to read the preceding four or five chapters to establish the setting in my mind.

King David had a son named Absalom, who had a sister named Tamar. Tamar was extremely beautiful and Absalom was the most handsome young man in the nation. He had his hair cut just once a year, but what was cut off weighed five pounds. Among the rest of the king's children, they had a half brother named Amon who became "lovesick" over Tamar.

His uncle gave him a plan to get Tamar alone in his house and he raped her, despite her protests. She told him that if he would just ask the king that the king would let him marry her, but he would not listen. Then he despised her and kicked her out of his house. She tore her clothes and put dirt on her head, which was a sign of mourning in those days.

As she walked down the road, she met her brother Absalom. He told her to be quiet, because Amon was her brother. He took her to his house and let her stay there. She lived "desolate." Eventually, Absalom got the opportunity to have his servants murder Amon. Then he ran away and hid from his father.

Joab, the captain of David's army, eventually had a woman come and tell King David a false story to convince him to have Absalom brought back to Jerusalem, because he could tell that the king was missing Absalom. The king had him brought back, but he would not see him. For two years he lived virtually under house arrest. Absalom tricked Joab into coming to see him, and then convinced him to persuade the king to restore him to fellowship. A pattern of Absalom's life after the rape of his sister was planning evil and trickery.

Immediately Absalom, being a prince, lined up fifty men to run ahead of him. In those days, people of important positions often had men to run ahead of them to announce their arrival. He got horses and chariots to ride in. Everywhere he went it was quite a show. Every day he went and stood by the gate to the city.

Anyone who came along that had a problem would encounter Absalom. He would yell and ask what city they were from. After they answered, Absalom would say, "See, thy matters are good and right; but there is no man deputed of the king to hear thee" (2 Samuel 15:3).

This was a lie. David always had time for the people. Evidence of this fact is the woman whom Joab sent to tell the false story to the king to benefit Absalom. Then Absalom would say, "Oh that I were made judge in the land, that every man which hath any suit or cause might come unto me, and I would do him justice!" (2 Samuel 15:4). He sat there and lied to the people day after day. If any man came to bow to him, as the custom was since he was a prince, he would lift him up and kiss him on the cheek, the way an equal was greeted in those days. He did this for forty years and stole the hearts of the people from his father, the king.

Then he told the king another lie, and he went and raised an army and was crowned king by this horde of rebels. Someone came and told David. He gathered up all of his household, except ten concubines who were left to take care of the house, and left town. Absalom and his gang showed up and took over the palace. The result of forty years of lying and planning rebellion came to pass.

A concubine was a female slave who was primarily responsible for having children to ensure the continuation of the family name. Concubines were considered wives, and their children could inherit the throne and royal property. They were considered to be special as a wife by the king.

Absalom's chief advisor, Ahithophel, told him to put a tent on the roof of the palace so the whole city of Jerusalem could see and sleep with his father's concubine. Then the people would think that there could be no reconciliation between David and Absalom. A son who sleeps with his father's concubine could not be forgiven easily. Then the people would feel that they had to choose who they were going to support.

Second Samuel 16:23 states: "And the counsel of Ahithophel,

which he counselled in those days, was as if a man had inquired at the oracle of God: so was all the counsel of Ahithophel both with David and with Absalom."

Ahithophel's advice was considered as good as God's Word by both David and Absalom. Ahithophel advised Absalom to let him choose twelve thousand men and go after David while he was tired from moving this huge group out of the palace. He would kill only David, and then all of the people would serve Absalom. This sounded good to Absalom and all the leaders of the people.

David, however, had an advisor, Hushai the Archite, who was loyal to him. He had already told Absalom that he would be loyal to whoever was in power. Absalom asked him what he thought. He said that Ahithophel's advice was not good this time.

He advised him to wait until every fighting man in the nation could be gathered together, and then pursue David wherever he went. With that mighty army they could get David no matter where he hid. He advised this because he said to Absalom in 2 Samuel 17:8: "Thou knowest thy father and his men, that they be mighty men, and they be chafed in their minds, as a bear robbed of her whelps in the field: and thy father is a man of war, and will not lodge with the people."

Everybody knows better than to mess with a mad mama bear. She will tear up anything that gets between her and her cubs. He went on to tell Absalom that when his army was being beaten by David's in the beginning of the battle that everyone would say that Absalom's army was being slaughtered. Then even the man who was as brave as a lion would melt with fear, because the whole nation would know that his father was a mighty man and his men were the bravest in the world. After this buildup of David by Hushai, Absalom was not about to go after his father until he could raise the biggest army possible.

Hushai sent a message to David to cross the river because he did not know for sure what Absalom would do, but Absalom feared his father and Hushai had made his point well: "And Absalom and all the men of Israel said, The counsel of Hushai the Archite is better than the counsel of Ahithophel..." (2 Samuel 17:14).

Hushai's advice was followed. Ahithophel went home, put his affairs in order, and hanged himself. Absalom gathered a mighty army and went out to fight his father's army. In the battle, Absalom's troops were soundly defeated and scattered. As he was fleeing on his mule, Absalom's famous hair got caught in an oak tree and his mule ran out from under him. He was left hanging from the tree by his hair.

When David's men got to Absalom, they refused to harm him because David had given strict instructions not to harm him. He was still his son. But Joab, captain of David's army, stuck three arrows through Absalom's heart. Then his ten personal armor-bearers gathered around Absalom and killed him.

After the Lord had me read this story every day for a week, He quoted one verse to me out of the eighth chapter of Romans: "If God be for us, who can be against us?" (Romans 8:31).

Absalom appeared to have the best advisor, the people on his side, and his dad on the run, but the key is found in 2 Samuel 17:14: "For the Lord had appointed to defeat the good counsel of Ahithophel, to the intent that he might bring evil upon Absalom."

It does not make any difference who or what is against us. If God is on our side, we win! Just as David defeated the lion, the bear, and Goliath with God on his side, he was brought back and restored to the throne. And even though he did all that he could to save Absalom, he was killed because of his evil ways.

If we have truly given our lives to Jesus, God is for us. We must be people of faith like David who ran towards Goliath. His right relationship with God gave him great faith.

If you have not given your life totally to Jesus, you can right now. Give Him your life by beginning to seek His will for your life. What does He desire for you to do with your life? When you really give your life to Jesus, you will desire to read and study the Bible continually. You will search for time and opportunities to pray. You will desire to know how you can serve God in the way that He desires. You will live and breathe to please Him in all you think, say, and do. If your relationship with God is not like this, it is His desire for it to be this way. If you begin to seek Him with all of your heart, soul, and mind, you will find Him. He will be for you like He was for David.

The word must be mixed with faith, but is there anything else that is needed to stay on the way like the pilgrim in *Pilgrim's Progress?*

CHAPTER SEVEN

POWER TO STAY ON THE
WAY IN EVIL TIMES

THE BIBLE TEACHES that as time goes on, the world will become more and more evil (2 Timothy 3:1–13). The result will be that many Christians' love for God will grow cold (Matthew 24:12). Many false teachers will come along and deceive many (Matthew 24:11). They will say things that the people like to hear (2 Timothy 4:3). This is in direct opposition to the example of biblical prophets and men of God who were generally hated by the leaders and many of the people.

These people will not accept the truth because they are driven by their own carnal desires (2 Timothy 4:3). God will give them great delusion to believe lies because of these selfish interpretations of God's Word (2 Timothy 4:4, 2 Thessalonians 2:11). Like Demas, the one-time disciple, they love this present world and the "good life" in it. They are concerned about how they live in this life rather than preparing for the next life. They deny this, but their actions show that their primary concern is not for the souls of other people, but the quality of their own life. They may speak of concern for others, be a regular worker in the church, do some acts of self-righteousness, and even give to the work of the church out of their abundance, but the work of God and pleasing Him are not the driving forces in their lives.

They need to learn that "whatsoever a man soweth, that shall he also reap. For he that soweth to his flesh shall of the flesh reap corruption; but he that soweth to the Spirit shall of the Spirit reap life everlasting" (Galatians 6:7–8). Also, the message of Matthew 6:33 is necessary to escape this trap. As time goes on, the financial pressure and stress of "making ends meet" is going to become bigger and bigger.

The true disciple of Jesus is instructed to take life one day at a time, because "sufficient unto the day is the evil thereof" (Matthew 6:34).

The strength of temptation to sin will become stronger and stronger. Movies, printed material, styles of dress, attitudes, common conduct of people, selfishness exhibited in every conceivable form, and the pressure to conform to this lifestyle will become stronger than ever in history, many times over. This process has been going on for some time already. It is going to greatly intensify in the future. Real Christians will be persecuted more than at anytime in Church history. Still, there have been some periods of strong persecution in the past.

How are we to find the strength to stay true to God in the days ahead? How are we going to resist temptation and endure persecution without shrinking back? Where will we find the power to be one of those in Revelation 12:11 who "loved not their lives unto the death"? This means that we must be ready to die for the testimony of Jesus and His truth.

This strength comes from maintaining that level of commitment to God that is complete, and that totally consumes our lives with the power of the Holy Spirit. Jesus taught the necessity of having the power of the Holy Spirit in the last days in the parable of the ten virgins in Matthew 25.

Matthew 24 establishes the time of this parable as just preceding the return of Jesus and the end of this world system, when Satan will be kept in the pit for a thousand years and Jesus will reign on earth. He told of many things that would happen just before His return. Also, He said that if those days of tribulation were not cut short, no flesh would survive on the earth. But for the sake of the elect (those called out of the world system to be in God's kingdom), those days would be cut short. Revelation speaks of one-third of all life on the earth being destroyed during that time.

He starts the parable of the ten virgins by saying "then" or "at that time." This establishes the time as the period just discussed. Matthew 25:1 states: "Then shall the kingdom of heaven be likened unto ten virgins, which took their lamps, and went forth to meet the bridegroom."

Notice that this is a parable about the kingdom of heaven (God's people). All ten were virgins saving themselves for the bridegroom (Jesus). All ten went out to wait for the bridegroom (separated themselves for the bridegroom). This establishes that these were all "Christians in the last days."

Matthew 25:2–4 states: "And five of them were wise, and five were foolish. They that were foolish took their lamps, and took no oil with them: But the wise took oil in their vessels with their lamps."

The difference between wisdom and foolishness was taking oil with them. Oil used in a figurative sense in the Bible always represents the Spirit of God. In the Old Testament they made anointing oil according to the recipe given to them by God in the law. They took this and poured it liberally over the head of the one being anointed. This was symbolic of being covered with the Spirit of God. Saul had the Spirit of God come on him until his disobedience caused the Spirit to leave him. Then he was tormented by an evil spirit, and David was brought to play the harp for him to give him some relief.

After David was anointed, the Spirit of God was upon him from that day forward (1 Samuel 16:13). Then he killed a lion and a bear with his hands. After that came his biggest test. It was a giant named Goliath. He was almost ten feet tall, and he wore a coat of mail (a shirt made of linen with overlapping brass plates attached) that weighed around 150 pounds. His spearhead weighed around eighteen pounds, and the whole spear probably weighed around twenty-five pounds.

Today's shot-putters are able to throw an eighteen-pound shot a maximum distance of about seventy-five feet. Javelins (spears) are thrown a maximum of around 340 feet. Goliath was so strong that he was throwing a spear that weighed approximately twenty-five pounds. The strength to throw a weapon of this weight against men throwing spears weighing five pounds or less is incredible. In close combat, quickness and accuracy are usually the deciding factors that determine who lives. Great strength and agility are needed in handling a twenty-five-pound weapon. He was the champion warrior.

Goliath towered over an average man, and especially a young man like David. For a young man like David to go out to fight this giant looked like pure suicide to everyone except David. While operating with the power of the Holy Spirit, David was as invincible as Samson had been with long hair. The Holy Spirit enabled men to do superhuman exploits throughout the Bible. Acts states that you will receive power after the Holy Ghost is come upon you (Acts 1:8). The power of the Holy Spirit will enable men to stand firm in the last days.

In this parable all ten virgins had their lamps. Lamps are used to produce light. Our light is the fruit of the Spirit, or the character of God, showing the nature of God to all with whom we come into contact. Oil is necessary to produce light in a lamp. Without the oil of the Holy Spirit, the light will not continue to show in our lives.

The word "vessel" is used to represent our bodies in several places in the New Testament (Acts 9:15, Romans 21–23, 2 Corinthians 4:7, 1 Thessalonians 4:4, 1 Timothy 2:20–21, 1 Peter 3:7). As we found in a previous chapter, the testimony of the book of Acts shows that the Holy Spirit is not received in this way at the time of "conversion." The nature of the spirit of the person is changed at conversion, but he does not always receive the power of the Holy Spirit at that time. Paul says that our bodies are temples of the Holy Spirit or the place where He lives. But the foolish virgins had no oil in their vessels.

Matthew 25:5 states: "While the bridegroom tarried, they all slumbered and slept." The bridegroom is because He is "not willing that any should perish, but that all should come to repentance" (2 Peter 3:9). There are several things for which He is waiting.

In Noah's day, "God saw that the wickedness of man was great in the earth, and that every imagination of the thoughts of his heart was only evil continually" (Genesis 6:5). Men were totally driven by selfish motives. All they did was for their own benefit. These people may have done a lot for others, but their motivation was what they received in return.

Free enterprise business operates this way. When they give, it is to gain a return of some kind. They are motivated by the lust of the flesh, the lust of the eyes, or the pride of life. What they do is motivated by the natural desires of their body (food, clothing, sex, etc.), what they see that they desire to possess, and/or their pride in who they are or what they have. These desires are never permanently satisfied. The Bible states that these three motivations, in all of their forms, are not from God. They are earthly and sensual (1 John 2:16).

God showed Abraham the land of Canaan and told him that it would belong to his descendants. He said that it would be later, because the sin of the Amorites was not yet full, as it was in the days of Noah. Jesus said that the meek would inherit the earth, but the sin of the earth in not yet full.

Jesus said that Jerusalem would be trodden down of the Gentiles until the times of the Gentiles be fulfilled. Although Jerusalem may still be a divided city, the nation of Israel has ruled over it since 1967. I believe that the Jews will take control of the temple mount and rebuild their temple in the near future. The priests are already trained, and the articles of worship are being made. When the Antichrist comes, he will stop the offering of the daily sacrifice at the temple. Then the period of Great Tribulation will start.

The parable takes place during this time. As they waited, they all "slumbered and slept." Paul says in Romans 14:11–12, "It is high time to awake out of sleep" and "cast off the works of darkness." In 1 Corinthians 15:34 he says, "Awake to righteousness, and sin not…" In Ephesians 5:14 he says, "Awake thou that sleepest, and arise from the dead, and Christ shall give thee light." Slumbering and sleeping allow your light to go down—the fruit of the Spirit, the works of Christ, and the power of the Holy Spirit—and are not evidenced in your life in the same way that they were in Jesus' life.

Matthew 25:6–7 states: "And at midnight there was a cry

made, Behold, the bridegroom cometh; go ye out to meet him. Then all those virgins arose, and trimmed their lamps."

When the cry was made, they had time to arise and trim their lamps but, as we will see, they did not have a lot of time to fool around. All ten trimmed their lamps. They attempted to get right with God, show the fruit of the Spirit in their lives, and do the works of Christ, but the five foolish virgins did not have the ability. They said, "We don't need that baptism in the Holy Spirit stuff, and we don't know if speaking in tongues is of God or not." They refused the gift of God.

Matthew 25:8–9 states: "And the foolish said unto the wise, Give us of your oil; for our lamps are gone out. But the wise answered, saying, Not so; lest there be not enough for us and you; but go ye rather to them that sell, and buy for yourselves."

A lamp without oil will not burn for very long. The light it gives will never become bright. If you have ever adjusted the wick on a kerosene lantern, you know that if it is out of kerosene, it will not burn brightly no matter how hard you try.

The foolish virgins said to the wise, "Give us some of your spirit," but the wise said, "No, you have to go to the source to get the oil." Will you not go to the source now and ask Jesus to baptize you with the Holy Spirit? Do not wait! Now is the time. God told us to call our ministry "In-Time Ministry." Will you not ask Him now while there is time? Jesus said the night comes when no man can work. There will be a time when it is too late.

Matthew 25:10–12 states: "And while they went to buy, the bridegroom came; and they that were ready went in with him to the marriage: and the door was shut. Afterward came also the other virgins, saying, Lord, Lord, open to us. But he answered and said, Verily, I say unto you, I know you not."

How terrible! They were all virgins (Christians). They all

went out to wait for Him (they wanted Him to return). Now He says that He does not know them! It is awful to live your whole life expecting to be received and then be refused.

> Not every one that saith unto me, Lord, Lord, shall enter into the kingdom of heaven; but he that doeth the will of my Father which is in heaven. Many will say to me in that day, Lord, Lord, have we not prophesied in thy name? and in thy name have cast out devils? and in thy name done many wonderful works? And then will I profess unto them, I never knew you: depart from me, ye that work iniquity.
>
> MATTHEW 7:21–23

You can preach the gospel, cast out devils, feed the hungry, clothe the naked, work for social reform, and do many other good things and still miss heaven. All of these are good works, but we must keep His commandments by abiding in His teaching, being careful to obey them (working out our own salvation with fear and trembling, Philippians 2:12), and being led by the Spirit.

Now, these are religious people who are not careful to love Him and obey His commandments. Maybe they do not turn the other cheek, or maybe they are concerned with the future as to what they will have to eat, drink, and wear. They are concerned about money and things (mammon). They have never learned to really live out Matthew 6:33. Will you not choose to trust God today and keep His commandments?

In the next chapter we will begin to learn about our new best friend and constant companion.

CHAPTER EIGHT

THE HOLY SPIRIT: GUIDE AND COMPANION ON THE WAY

SPIRITUAL EXPERIENCES are among the most profound to effect change that many people can have. In my own life, just as in millions of others, my spiritual experience completely changed the direction and course of my life and the lives of the members of my family. As I shared earlier, the change was so drastic as to cause my brother-in-law, who knew me very well, to look at me after only a couple of weeks and say, "I don't know you anymore."

The change was instantaneous. I did not think the same thoughts anymore. I did not say the same things anymore. I was submitted to God in my heart and it showed in every area of my life.

Many people have spiritual experiences involving many different spirits, but we will consider only the Holy Spirit of God. He is the part of God who is present with us in the world. We will use the Bible and personal experience to study teachings about, and examples of, the interactions of the Spirit of God with people.

The Greek word *pneuma* is translated into English as ghost, life, spirit. It literally means a current of air, a breath (blast) or a breeze. It comes from the Greek word *pneo,* meaning to breathe.

Jesus compared the Spirit to the wind, just as the word literally means a current of air. We cannot normally see Him, but we can detect His presence by what He does (John 3). Just as the air is always present but not always moving, the Spirit is always present but not always noticed.

John 16:7 states: "Nevertheless I tell you the truth; It is expedient for you that I go away: for if I go not away, the Comforter will not come unto you; but if I depart, I will sent him unto you."

The Comforter is the Holy Spirit (John 14:26). The Holy Spirit could not come to live inside of people until Jesus died to take away the sin of the world. The Holy Spirit could not have that kind of communion with people because they were separated from God by their sin (Isaiah 59:1).

The Bible says that Jesus became sin so that we might be made the righteousness of God (2 Corinthians 5:21). To be righteous is to be blameless. It is the state of being in a perfect relationship with God or without sin. Sin is breaking the law of God (1 John 3:4). Jesus paid the price for the sin of the whole of mankind. Now we can be reconciled to God because of the sacrifice of Jesus. He died for our sins, not His own, so the Spirit of God can have communion with us without becoming defiled, even though we have sinned. Our sins are forgiven when we believe in our heart that God raised Jesus from the dead and confess with our mouths that He is Lord of our life (Romans 10:9–10). We are then eligible candidates to receive the Holy Spirit.

Jesus said that no one could truly surrender his life to Him unless the Father draws him (John 6:65). The Holy Spirit draws people to Jesus when the cross is preached. He does that first of all by making them aware of their need.

John 16:8 states: "And when he is come, he will reprove the world of sin, and of righteousness, and of judgment."

The Bible shows in Genesis that God created man perfect. Man became sinful through obedience to the devil, who has been opposed to God for a long time. Romans 6:16 says, "Know ye not, that to whom ye yield yourselves servants to obey, his servants ye are to whom ye obey; whether of sin unto death, or of obedience unto righteousness?" Man became a servant of the devil by obeying him. Those who sin are not righteous, and those who are not righteous will face judgment. Those who face judgment, while unrighteous, will be condemned. John 16:9 states, "Of sin, because they believe not on me."

Jesus said, "I am the way, the truth, and the life: no man cometh unto the Father, but by me" (John 14:6). The Holy Spirit convicts people of their sinful condition when they have not given their lives to Jesus. Those who believe and surrender their lives to Him are freed from that conviction when they surrender to Him. John 16:10 states, "Of righteousness, because I go to my Father, and ye see me no more."

The resurrection of Jesus from the dead and His ascension into heaven prove His righteousness. The Bible says, "The wages of sin is death" (Romans 6:23). Sin produces death. This is a matter of natural consequence. When Adam and Eve ate the fruit of the tree of the knowledge of good and evil, spiritual death occurred immediately. This is separation from the source of all life (God). Physical death started then and consummated some years later. The fact that Jesus was taken to heaven proves His righteousness. The Holy Spirit convicts people of their lack of righteousness, which will prevent them from going to heaven. John 16:11 states, "Of judgment, because the prince of this world is judged."

Satan has already been judged and found guilty. He is on death row awaiting the execution of his sentence. That is not an entirely accurate analogy. His sentence has been announced, but he is not being held prisoner at this time. He was thrown out of heaven at the announcement of his verdict. At the end of the millennial reign with Jesus on the earth, he will be thrown into the lake of fire that is made for him and his followers.

The devil's transgression was to rebel against the authority of God. The sentence was eternal separation from God (death). In the Bible this is called the second death. All of those who follow the example of the devil will receive the same sentence. The wages or earnings of sin are death (Romans 6:23). The redeemed are exceptions to this.

Most of the Church has long held the doctrine of original sin in one form or another. This doctrine says that people are born with the natural tendency to sin. Close observation of very young children is enough to substantiate this doctrine. Children must be taught not to be selfish. Many are never taught this.

In fact, without a spiritual change and the steady influence of God's Word in their lives, the change will never be complete. Society makes many attempts to train children not to be selfish in some ways, but a mixed signal is given.

While speaking unselfishness about some things, we ask our children what they desire to do with their lives. We ask them what they want for their birthday and then we are upset when they cry and yell when they do not get what they desire. We spoil our children in an effort to demonstrate our love.

This is because we, as parents, do not understand what real mature love does. Mature love does what is best for the object loved, while respecting their individuality. The Bible says that the parent who spares the rod hates his child (Proverbs 13:24). The reason is that the result of no discipline is uncontrolled behavior. Adults with uncontrolled behavior are imprisoned in every society on earth. Insufficient discipline produces uncontrolled behavior to the degree that needed discipline is not applied.

Some people have what appears to be a stronger spirit of rebellion than others. Discipline will keep it under control, but it will not do away with it. A spiritual change is required to eliminate it from a person's life. A spiritual change may be temporary. It has to be maintained.

In addition, knowledge of right and wrong must be attained before it can be practiced. This comes from renewing the mind (Romans 12:1–2).

The Holy Spirit is involved in the spiritual change by using the Word of God when it is spoken, written, or by the actions of a righteous person. Knowledge of Jesus is required for a person to believe in Him. Real belief in Jesus will cause the spiritual change at that time. Failure to keep a person's eye single (Matthew 6:22–23) will allow the spirit of rebellion to be present in that person's life to whatever degree the eye is not single. The work of the Holy Spirit is to make that person aware of his backslidden condition. Once again, He uses the Word of God, whether spoken, written, or demonstrated to convict the sinner of his sinfulness.

When a "Christian" is not totally submitted to God in his heart, striving to please Him in all that he thinks, says, and does, he is backslidden. Also, to live for the benefit of the physical body or any other selfish motivation is to be backslidden. To be backslidden is to be turned back from the state of true conversion, which is the total consecration of one's self to God and to His service.

Anyone in this condition is a candidate for the conviction of the Holy Spirit of one's sin. Either submission to the conviction of the Holy Spirit occurs at that time or one becomes hardened in heart by resisting the will of God. With time one may become so hardened as not to even feel convicted at any time by any action of the Holy Spirit, or even one's own conscience.

If you are not living for Jesus, will you not surrender your life to Him right now? Cease seeking your own dreams and goals, and seek the kingdom of God and His righteousness (Matthew 6:33). If you will give your life to Him totally, you are a candidate for the next action of the Holy Spirit, which is to come and live with you. He desires an ever-present, intimate relationship with you. He wants to talk to you. He wants to teach you. He wants to show you the way to go in your life. He wants only the best for you.

John 14:15–18 states: "If you love me, keep my commandments, And I will pray the Father, and he shall give you another Comforter, that he may abide with you for ever; Even the Spirit of truth; whom the world cannot receive, because it seeth him not, neither knoweth him: but ye know him; for he dwelleth with you, and shall be in you. I will not leave you comfortless: I will come to you."

The promise of the Father is for those who love Jesus and keep His commandments. He desires to live in them. They are called the tabernacle of the Holy Spirit or the dwelling of God in the earth. He does not live just in a building in Jerusalem anymore. He lives in people.

John 16:13 states: "Howbeit when he, the Spirit of truth, is come, he will guide you into all truth: for he shall not speak of himself; but whatsoever he shall hear, that shall he speak: and he will shew you things to come."

The Holy Spirit does not initiate the things that He says, but He is the messenger of God. God is not a man that He should lie

(Numbers 23:19), so the Spirit only speaks the truth. He is not the only spirit in the world, but Jesus said that His sheep know His voice and the voice of a stranger they will not follow.

If our lives are really submitted to Jesus and we are keeping His commandments, we will know the voice of the Holy Spirit, which is very easy to distinguish. He never says anything in opposition to the written Word of God.

When does the Holy Spirit begin to live in a person? Is it at the time of conversion as many people teach? Is the Holy Spirit a thing of the past? If not, who has the Holy Spirit? How do we know?

Acts 1:4–5 states: "And, being assembled together with them, command them that they should not depart from Jerusalem, but wait for the promise of the Father, which, saith he, ye have heard of me. For John truly baptized with water; but ye shall be baptized with the Holy Ghost not many days hence."

Baptism in water is the baptism of repentance (John 3:3, Acts 19:3–4). The result of repentance is the remission of sins. This was true in Old Testament times. Ezekiel 33:14–16 states: "Again, when I say unto the wicked, Thou shalt surely die; if he turn from his sin, and do that which is lawful and right; If the wicked restore the pledge, give again that he had robbed, walk in the statutes of life, without committing iniquity; he shall surely live, he shall not die. None of his sins that he hath committed shall be mentioned unto him: he hath done that which is lawful and right; he shall surely live."

Repentance is to turn from sin and do that which is lawful and right. Repentance is also a New Testament message (Acts 2:38). But even in the Old Testament days, if a person repented and did that which was right, none of his sins were mentioned to him. They were remitted.

Jesus brought the baptism of the Holy Spirit. This was not available before His ascension. The Spirit of God inhabited the Holy of Holies in the temple of Jerusalem, but the veil in the temple split when Jesus died and the Spirit of God came out. Then, on the day of Pentecost, He came to the apostles: "But ye shall receive power, after that the Holy Ghost is come upon you: and ye shall be witnesses unto me both in Jerusalem, and in all Judea, and in Samaria, and unto the uttermost part of the earth" (Acts 1:8).

The Greek word *dunamis* is translated into English as "power," which means force, miraculous power: ability, abundance, meaning, might, (worker of) miracles, strength, violence, mighty (wonderful) work. The English words "dynamo" and "dynamite" are derived from this root word. A dynamo generates electricity (power). Dynamite obviously has much power. If it is controlled, it is useful, but if uncontrolled, it is very dangerous.

Jesus said that when the Holy Spirit abides with a person, he has great working power in him. This is the same power that raised Jesus from the dead (Romans 8:11). This is the same power that created everything that exists. This is the same power that enabled Jesus to open blind eyes, raise the dead, walk on water, multiply the loaves and fishes, and live a life pleasing to God in every way. He said that those baptized in the Holy Spirit have this power in them. It is the power of Almighty God. Nothing can stand against it. It is limitless power. Jesus said all things are possible to him who believes (Mark 9:23, 11:22–24).

There is a saying in the world that is true: "Power corrupts and absolute power corrupts absolutely." This is true of everyone who is given power without being submitted to authority. Therefore, God does not give this power to anyone who is not submitted to Jesus' authority. This power is never available to people to possess as in ownership, but it is available to work for them.

"And Jesus came and spake unto them, saying, All power is given unto me in heaven and in earth" (Matthew 28:18). As we have previously shown, the word "power" in this verse means authority as that of a king, meaning complete. Only those who are subject to the authority of Jesus can exercise the power of the Holy Spirit.

In John 9:33, the man who was born blind whom Jesus healed makes a strong and very truthful statement to the Pharisees: "If this man were not of God, he could do nothing." The power of the Holy Spirit is available only to those who are subject to the will of God. It is His will that we should believe in Jesus and keep His commandments. It is also His will that we should receive the gift of the Holy Spirit.

> And when the day of Pentecost was fully come, they were all with one accord in one place. And suddenly there came a sound from heaven as of a rushing mighty wind, and it filled all the house where they were sitting. And there appeared unto them cloven tongues like as of fire, and it sat upon each of them. And they were all filled with the Holy Ghost, and began to speak with other tongues, as the Spirit gave them utterance.
>
> ACTS 2:1-4

When the Holy Spirit came on the day of Pentecost, they heard Him and saw Him sit on each of them. When they were all filled with the Holy Spirit, they spoke in other languages as the Spirit moved them and gave them utterance. This was the promise of God. The prophet Joel spoke of it and Jesus spoke of this event. This was the first installment of the fulfillment of this prophecy.

Acts 2:32–33 states: "This Jesus hath God raised up, whereof we all are witnesses. Therefore being by the right hand of God exalted, and having received of the Father the promise of the Holy Spirit, he hath shed forth this, which ye now see and hear."

Jesus received the Holy Spirit from the Father and sent Him into the world to live in people. He came to fill their lives and the evidence was the utterance that He gave them. These were the words of God being spoken by men (John 16:13). Their minds had no part in determining what they would say, because they spoke words that their minds did not understand (1 Corinthians 14:14). All of this came from God.

People from all over the known world at that time were present, and they all heard them speaking in their own language. They noticed that they were all Galileans and were amazed by what they saw and heard.

> Now when they heard this, they were pricked in their heart, and said unto Peter and to the rest of the apostles, Men and brethren, what shall we do? Then Peter said unto them, Repent, and be baptized every one of you in the name Jesus Christ for the remission of sins, and ye shall receive the gift of the Holy Ghost. For the promise is unto you, and to your children, and to all that are afar off, even as many as the Lord our God shall call.
>
> ACTS 2:37-39

The promise is to all—even that are afar off. This promise is for everyone whom God calls and is baptized in the name of Jesus for the remission of sins.

Baptism is an outward sign that the one being baptized has died to a life of sin and has been raised to walk (live) a new life that is controlled by the teachings and Spirit of Christ (Romans 6). This indicates the death and burial of the person that formerly inhabited that body. A new person lives in that body who is forgiven of past sins and who will now live a life in accordance with the teachings of Jesus while being led by His Spirit.

The Spirit is available to all who repent, stop breaking God's law (Ezekiel 33), and ask for the gift of the Holy Spirit. Luke 11:13 states: "If ye then, being evil, know how to give good gifts unto your children: how much more shall your heavenly Father give the Holy Spirit to them that ask him?"

The promise is to all who repent and are baptized in the name of Jesus. It is God's will for everyone to receive the gift of the Holy Spirit. He is not willing that any should perish (2 Peter 3:9), and He gets no pleasure in the death of the wicked (Ezekiel 33:11). It is God's desire that everyone would receive the gift of the Holy Spirit, but not everyone is willing to repent and be baptized in the name of Jesus, and not everyone is willing to accept the gift of the Father.

It is an amazing thing that many people will not accept the gift of salvation (the remission of sins), and an equally amazing thing how many people will accept the gift of salvation but not the gift of the Holy Spirit. He is for every member of the "elect" (the called out ones). Remember, no one comes to Jesus unless they are drawn by the Holy Spirit, but not everyone who is drawn gives their life to Jesus.

Some people teach that everyone who believes and is baptized receives the Holy Spirit. Others teach that while that is true, there is a second experience available which is described in Acts 2—the baptism in the Holy Spirit. Let's look at the examples given in the book of Acts to see what they reveal about this question.

Acts, chapter 8, contains the account of Philip going down

to Samaria to preach Jesus to the people. Verse twelve says that the people believed in Jesus and were baptized. When the apostles in Jerusalem heard about this, they sent Peter and John to see about it.

Acts 8:15–17 states: "Who, when they were come down, prayed for them, that they might receive the Holy Ghost: (For as yet he was fallen upon none of them: only they were baptized in the name of the Lord Jesus.) Then laid they their hands on them, and they received the Holy Ghost."

They did not receive the Holy Spirit when they believed, but they were baptized in the name of Jesus. It had to have been sometime later, because Peter and John had to travel to Samaria, probably on foot, which was a pretty fair distance to travel by walking. The Samaritans received the Holy Spirit when Peter and John prayed for them and laid their hands on them.

Acts, chapter 10, tells the story of a man named Cornelius who was a Roman centurion of the "Italian band." He was a devout man who feared God, along with his entire household, and prayed to God always. He also gave a lot of charity. He had a vision about three in the afternoon in which an angel told him to send for Peter, who was staying at Simon the tanner's house in Joppa.

Just as the men whom Cornelius sent arrived to get Peter, Peter had a vision in which God showed him that some of the things that had been considered unclean were no longer unclean. Anyone who was not a descendant of Abraham through Isaac was called a Gentile and was considered unclean (prohibited by Mosaic Law from having close association with). Israelites were not allowed to eat certain animals or to eat with people who were Gentiles. They considered Gentiles as ostracized by God, which to a great degree was very true.

When a Syrophenician woman came to Jesus to ask him to heal her daughter, He ignored her and then called her a dog. He said that He was only sent to the lost sheep of the house of Israel. No one had promises from God except the descendants of Abraham through Isaac. Paul wrote to the Ephesians and said that they were previously in the world without God and without hope. Even today, many Jews still believe this to be true. This experience proved to Peter that this was no longer true.

The Spirit told him to go with the men to Cornelius' house. When he got there he preached Jesus to the people gathered to hear him.

> While Peter yet spake these words, the Holy Ghost fell on all them which heard the word. And they of the circumcision which believed were astonished, as many as came with Peter, because that on the Gentiles also was poured out the gift of the Holy Ghost. For they heard them speak with tongues, and magnify God. Then answered Peter, Can any man forbid water, that these should not be baptized, which have received the Holy Ghost as well as we? And he commanded them to be baptized in the name of the Lord. Then prayed they him to tarry certain days.
>
> ACTS 10:44-48

The way they knew that they had received the Holy Spirit was by hearing them speak in tongues and magnify God. The Jews were astonished that God would give the Holy Spirit to Gentiles, but they knew that He had because they heard them speak with tongues.

Speaking in tongues is almost always the evidence of receiving the Holy Spirit. The power of the Holy Spirit may be demonstrated in many ways in a person's life, but tongues are almost always the initial evidence of having received the Holy Spirit.

In this case, the people received the Holy Spirit when they heard the Word about Jesus and the Kingdom of God, but it was evidenced by speaking in tongues. They were baptized after receiving the Holy Spirit.

There are two separate operations of the Holy Spirit in the life of the believer concerning tongues. One is the giving of a message from God to a body of believers and the interpretation of that message in the common language of the people (1 Corinthians 14). The other is commonly called the prayer language.

The prayer language is employed just as in the case of these people in Cornelius' house. Obviously, they were not giving a message in so many words to a body of believers as in a church. They must have all spoken at the same time. What they said was a sign to the people present, but not in so many words. It was simply showing to Peter and those with him that God was including the Gentiles in His kingdom.

This did not happen just for the benefit of Peter and those with him, but also for those who received the gift. The Jews learned from this, but the ones who received benefited from this directly.

In 1 Corinthians 14:13–15, Paul said that when a man speaks in tongues, he edifies himself: "Wherefore let him that speaketh in an unknown tongue pray that he may interpret. For if I pray in an unknown tongue, my spirit prayeth, but my understanding is unfruitful. What is it then? I will pray with the spirit, and I will pray with the understanding also: I will sing with the Spirit, and I will sing with the understanding also."

Notice that praying in an unknown tongue is identified as praying in the Spirit. Also, it shows that the person praying does not understand the words he is praying. The same thing is true of singing in the Spirit.

The other operation of the Spirit in the area of tongues is the giving of a message from God to a body of believers. The Spirit moves a person to speak a message to those present, and moves to give the interpretation to the same one or to another person who is present. The interpretation may or may not be a word for word translation in the common language of those present. In every case it is relating the message in the language of those present. Paul speaks of this in the twelfth chapter, and gives instructions about the orderly performance of it in the fourteenth chapter.

There are many operations of the Holy Spirit through people listed in 1 Corinthians 12 besides tongues and interpretation. They are the word of wisdom, word of knowledge, gifts of healings, faith, working of miracles, prophecy, and discerning of spirits. These are all given at the discretion of the Holy Spirit for the benefit of the members of the Body of Christ (the Church). Paul instructs us to earnestly covet, or seek, the best gifts or operations of the Spirit. We are not to just sit back and say, "If God wants me to have it, He will give it to me." We are to seek the gifts. We are to covet the Holy Spirit's operation in our lives.

In this chapter Paul very vividly points out that each member of the body needs the other members. Just because they may have a different operation of the Spirit in their life does not mean that we do not need them. We all need the operation of the Spirit in our lives.

In Romans 8:9 Paul says, "Now if any man have not the Spirit of Christ, he is none of his." In Romans 8:5 he says, "For they that are after the flesh do mind the things of the flesh; but they that are after the Spirit the things of the Spirit."

The word translated "mind" in Romans 8:5 means to interest one's self with. Those that interest themselves with the things of the flesh do not belong to Jesus. The things of the flesh are the needs and desires of the natural, carnal nature of people. Those who live desiring and pursuing those things are not after, or led by, the Spirit of Christ. They do not belong to Him. We need the operation of the Spirit in our lives.

In Romans 8:14 Paul says, "For as many as are led by the Spirit of God, they are the sons of God." If we are being led by the Holy Spirit, the evidence will be produced in our lives. We will look at this evidence in the next chapter.

CHAPTER NINE

EVIDENCE THAT WE ARE ON THE WAY

TONGUES ARE THE initial evidence of the Spirit's involvement in a person's life, but we must look at the evidence of the Spirit's control of a person's life. Romans 8:9 says, "Now if any man have not the Spirit of Christ, he is none of his." The Spirit of Christ, the Spirit of God, and the Spirit of truth are all used interchangeably in the New Testament. Jesus told Thomas that there was no difference between Himself and the Father. If you have seen one, you have seen the other.

Paul goes on to say, "For as many as are led by the Spirit of God, they are the sons of God" (Romans 8:14). To be led by the Spirit is to have our lives directed and controlled by Him. But how can we know if this is really happening?

Second Corinthians 13:5 says, "Examine yourselves, whether ye be in the faith; prove your own selves. Know ye not your own selves, how that Jesus Christ is in you, except ye be reprobates?" We are to examine ourselves and look at our own lives. How do we measure up?

First Corinthians 11:31–32 states: "For if we would judge ourselves, we should not be judged. But when we are judged, we are chastened of the Lord, that we should not be condemned with the world."

If we will judge ourselves, God will not have to judge us. If God does judge us, He will discipline us to correct our behavior so that we will do what is right and not be condemned with the world. So let us judge ourselves.

Jesus said to enter at the straight gate because straight is the gate and narrow is the way that leads to life (Matthew 7:13–14). We have looked at signs that show that we are not on the narrow way that leads to life. Now let's look at the signs that show that we are being led by the Spirit, and that we are on the straight and narrow way that leads to life.

Galatians 5:22–23 states: "But the fruit of the Spirit is love, joy, peace, longsuffering, gentleness, goodness, faith, Meekness, temperance: against such there is no law."

The first and most important sign is love. "Though I speak with the tongues of men and of angels, and have not charity (love), I am become as sounding brass, or a tinkling cymbal" (1 Corinthians 13:1). Speaking in tongues edifies a person and is good, but to be filled with the love of God that causes us to love our fellow man is more important.

"And though I have the gift of prophecy, and understand all mysteries, and all knowledge; and though I have all faith, so that I could remove mountains, and have not charity (love), I am nothing" (1 Corinthians 13:2). The gifts of prophecy, wisdom, and great faith are all very important in the kingdom of heaven, but they are built on love. Without love, all of the rest of the gifts are totally unprofitable. They are worthless unless they are controlled and motivated by love.

"And though I bestow all my goods to feed the poor, and though I give my body to be burned, and have not charity (love), it profiteth me nothing" (1 Corinthians 13:3). Giving must be an act of compassion and love. We can give everything that we have but, if our motivation is selfish, it profits us nothing. Acts of charity must be motivated by love, not greed or selfish gain.

"Love is patient…" (1 Corinthians 13:4, NIV). If we are filled with God's love, we are not impatient with other people. We are always ready to wait on others in whatever way is needed. Our patience shows in our attitude, words, and actions.

"Love is kind…" (1 Corinthians 13:4, NIV). If we are filled with God's love, we are gentle and considerate of other people. We do not purposefully do anything to hurt others.

"It does not envy…" (1 Corinthians 13:4, NIV). If we are filled with God's love, we do not say like the song, "I wish I had your good looks, charm, and you had a wack-a-do, wack-a-do, wack-a-do." We do not desire to be in the place of others, but we rejoice over the good fortune of others. We are happy for others when things go well for them, not desirous of their good position in life.

"It does not boast…" (1 Corinthians 13:4, NIV). If we are filled with God's love, we do not brag about ourselves; we build others up. Love always puts others ahead of one's self. It does not meditate on the qualities of itself.

"It is not proud" (1 Corinthians 13:4, NIV). If we are filled with God's love, we are not filled with pride that comes from boasting and meditating on our own goodness. We are humble, knowing that there is none good, save one, and that is God. All of our goodness is because of Him.

"It is not rude…" (1 Corinthians 13:5, NIV). If we are filled with God's love, we are never inconsiderate, selfish, or arrogant in our attitude, words, or actions.

"It is not self-seeking…" (1 Corinthians 13:5, NIV). If we are filled with God's love, we do not spend our life seeking our own good, profit, and advantage. Our life becomes dedicated to the service of others without being motivated by selfishness.

"It is not easily angered…" (1 Corinthians 13:5, NIV). If we are filled with God's love, we are not easily angered. Many times anger comes out of selfishness and a lack of patience. If we are patient, kind, and not envious, we are not likely to be easily angered.

"It keeps no record of wrongs" (1 Corinthians 13:5, NIV). If we are filled with God's love, we are quick to forgive and not hold grudges. Jesus said that if we do not forgive our fellowman, we will not be forgiven by God. A person filled with the Spirit of God is quick to forgive and does not rehearse offenses that they have endured in an unforgiving way.

"Love does not delight in evil but rejoices with the truth" (1 Corinthians 13:6, NIV). If we are filled with God's love, we do not enjoy seeing bad things happen. We do not enjoy movies or other forms of entertainment that depict death, violence, immorality, and the like. We do not enjoy evil prevailing over good. We enjoy seeing the love of God prevail over evil. We do not enjoy seeing people "get what they have coming," but we love mercy and forgiveness. We are like God, who gets no pleasure in the death of the wicked, but rather that they would repent and receive forgiveness.

"It always protects…" (1 Corinthians 13:7, NIV). If we are filled with God's love, we do not try to expose the wrongs or mistakes of other people; we protect them, not to condone their wrong, but to the Lord judge them. Vengeance belongs to Him.

Love "always trusts…" (1 Corinthians 13:7, NIV). If we are filled with God's love, we expect good and not evil. We are disappointed if others do wrong, because we did not expect it. We are looking for the best in others, not the worst. We speak positively about them. We encourage and build them up, rather than discourage and tear them down. If we are filled with the same Spirit as Jesus, this is our nature.

Love "always hopes…" (1 Corinthians 13:7, NIV). If we are filled with God's love, we maintain hope for a good outcome. We know that with God all things are possible, and it's not over till it's over. Even when it appears to be over, it is not over with God. This fact was made evident when Jesus raised Lazarus from the dead after he had been dead for four days. God is the one who made the rules of nature; therefore, they are not an obstacle to Him. It is easy for Him to be supernatural. We can have hope because nothing is impossible with God.

Love "always perseveres" (1 Corinthians 13:7, NIV). If we are filled with God's love, we are filled with hope that allows us to persevere. There is no reason to quit when we still have hope.

"Love never fails…" (1 Corinthians 13:8, NIV). If we are filled with God's love, we will not quit and we cannot fail.

I know a man who played defensive tackle in college football in the early 1950s. He told me about playing against a quarterback who passed the ball on almost every play. It was my friend's job to tackle the quarterback.

During the first half the quarterback always threw the ball before they were able to tackle him, but they knocked him down every play anyway. They really rubbed his nose in the dirt. Later, he was one of the smallest quarterbacks to play professional football. Both defensive tackles weighed about one hundred pounds more than the little quarterback.

Each time they knocked him down after he threw the ball, he would jump up, smile, reach down and help those big defensive tackles to their feet. At halftime my friend told the other defensive tackle that he was not going to hit the little guy anymore because he was just too nice! Love never fails! The little guy overcame evil with good. They still did their job, but they did not hit him after he threw the ball anymore.

After the Civil War Abraham Lincoln started reaching out to restore and rebuild the South. A northern senator asked him why he was reaching out to the South. He asked Abraham Lincoln if he did not know that we are supposed to destroy our enemies. Abraham Lincoln replied, "If I make a friend out of my enemy, haven't I destroyed my enemy?" Love never fails!

Love is the first sign that we are on the correct path. Now we will examine the next sign.

Joy

The Greek word *chara* is translated into English as "joy." It means cheerfulness, calm delight. It is not a joy that comes from rejoicing with evil, such as comes from seeing a mean joke played on someone. The Bible says, "Like a madman shooting firebrands or deadly arrows is a man who deceives his neighbor and says, 'I was only joking!'" (Proverbs 26:18–19, NIV). Proverbs 10:23 (NIV) says, "A fool finds pleasure in evil conduct, but a man of understanding delights in wisdom."

The joy that comes from the Spirit of God does not come from cruel jokes or evil behavior. The state of cheerfulness is not temporary; it is continuous as a result of living in a righteous relationship with God. The peace that passes all understanding and the faith that says, "Yea, though I walk through the valley of the shadow of death, I will fear no evil…" (Psalm 23:4), gives us this joy that cannot be taken away. A person may be burdened for a person, a group of people, or even for the world, yet there was a deep joy that allowed Paul and Silas to sing praises to God after being beaten and imprisoned.

Peace

The Greek word *eirene* is translated into English as "peace," and it probably comes from a primitive verb *eiro*, which means to join. Webster defines "peace" as a state of tranquility or quiet; it is freedom from disquieting or oppressive thoughts or emotions. Being joined with God, or being one with God, gives us this state of peace.

Jesus said, "And he that sent me is with me: the Father hath not left me alone, for I do always those things that please him" (John 8:29). If all that we think, say, and do is pleasing to the Father, we will stay joined to Him and He will not leave us. Then we have the peace that passes all understanding. We can be passing through the valley of the shadow of death and still have that peace.

This intimate relationship with the Holy Spirit produces an attitude like Jesus'. In the middle of the night He and the disciples were in a boat out in the Sea of Galilee. After a violent storm began, the disciples woke Jesus up from his slumber in the back of the boat. They asked Him if He cared that they were all going to die. He responded by asking them, "Why are ye so fearful? how is it that ye have no faith?" (Mark 4:40).

In the middle of the night, in the middle of the Sea of Galilee, and in the middle of a very violent storm, Jesus had perfect peace because of His relationship with the Holy Spirit. Remember, this relationship was a result of the belief and practice that "I do always those things that please him" (John 8:29).

Longsuffering

The Greek word *makrothumia* is translated into English as "long-suffering." It means longanimity, fortitude. Webster defines "longanimity" as a disposition to bear injuries patiently. This is the opposite of the desire to get back at those who do things that displease us. There is no desire for revenge or to see them get what they have coming.

While hanging on the cross, Jesus prayed and asked the Father to forgive those who crucified Him. I believe that He "suffers with us for a long time." We hurt Him a lot with the way that we think, speak, and act.

Gentleness

The Greek word *chrestotes* is translated into English as "gentleness." It means usefulness, moral excellence (in character or demeanor). People who are excellent in God's sight are useful. Even in our language, we use the term "gentlemen." Gentle men, or men who have gentleness, are useful to God and to people. Gentleness produces healing in those who will receive it. It produces calm in those who will receive it. It really is useful.

Goodness

The Greek word *agathosune* is translated into English as "goodness," which means virtue or beneficence. It is being a benefit, not a detriment. A detriment wears away or causes hurt or injury. Goodness is evidenced by restoring, repairing, protecting, or maintaining. Goodness is the state of having good character qualities.

Faith

The Greek word *pistis* is translated into English as "faith." It means persuasion, credence, moral conviction (of religious truth, or the truthfulness of God or a religious teacher), especially reliance upon Christ for salvation. If the blood of Jesus has put us into a right relationship with God and we are pleasing Him in all that we think, say, and do, we can have a relationship with the Holy Spirit that will produce faith in our hearts. First John says that if we keep His commandments, we have confidence with God. We expect Him to back up what we say by performing the things that we ask.

This faith allows us to go through life without fear in any and all situations. It is a calm assuredness that carries us through any problem or difficulty. This faith is more valuable than silver and gold. Silver and gold will only acquire what people can do for you, but faith will acquire for you what God can do, and that is more than we could ever think or ask.

Meekness

The Greek word *praotes* is translated into English as "meekness." It means gentleness and, by implication, humility. It is the state of not being proud or haughty. It is not thinking more highly of ourselves than we should. It is not attempting to build ourselves up in our own eyes or in the eyes of others for the sake of pride.

The Bible says that Moses was the meekest man on the earth. This is in spite of the fact that he was raised to be the next ruler of the most powerful and richest nation on earth. His meekness is shown by his reaction to God telling him to go talk to

Pharaoh. His answer was to ask who he was that he should go talk to Pharaoh.

When it came time to crown Saul king over Israel, he could not be found. He was hiding. This is in spite of the fact that he was head and shoulders taller than any other person in the whole nation. It is a pity that later he became proud.

When God spoke to Gideon about throwing off the rule of the Midianites, he was hiding by the winepress trying to thresh some wheat without getting caught. The angel of the Lord called him a brave man, and told him to defeat the Midianites. Gideon replied that his family was poor, his tribe was small, and who was he to do a job like that? He did not say, "Yes, I am the man for the job."

> For ye see your calling, brethren, how that not many wise men after the flesh, not many mighty, not many noble, are called: But God hath chosen the foolish things of the world to confound the wise; and God hath chosen the weak things of the world to confound the things which are mighty; And base things of the world, and things which are despised, hath God chosen, yea, and things which are not, to bring to nought things that are: That no flesh should glory in his presence.
>
> 1 CORINTHIANS 1:26–29

The knowledge of God makes us aware of how really unimportant we are. Furthermore, He chooses the ones who know that they are nobody without Him. This is so no flesh can glory in His presence. We should know what we are without God.

Temperance

The Greek word *enkrateia* is translated into English as "temperance." It means self-control. Paul said that he kept his body under subjection (1 Corinthians 9:27). This means that he ruled over his body and its natural desires. His stomach did not tell him what he was to get for it, but he told his stomach what it was going to get. His eyes did not tell him what he was going to get that they wanted; he told them what they were going to look at. He did not allow his natural desires to dictate his life. He was not ruled by cravings or immoral desires.

Desires that are fed will grow in strength; they do not weaken. Desires that are starved are the ones that weaken. If a person eats too much, they will develop a much bigger appetite. It gets bigger because it is fed more than it needs. This is not meant for condemnation but for freedom. Our desire is not to cause feelings of guilt, but to provide knowledge to help people become free from things that have controlled them against their will. Many people who have a desire that is controlling their life want to be free from its control.

The Lord will free you from anything that controls your life against your will. Jesus came to set the captives free. Simply ask the Lord to set you free. If you need help, seek out people of God who believe, and they will help you get free.

The important thing to know is that as we draw near to God by praying, reading His Word, and praising Him for His love and magnificence, He will draw near to us and set us free. Then, as we live in constant fellowship with the Holy Spirit, we will stay free. As the old song says, "The things of this world grow strangely dim in the light of His glory and grace." As we grow closer to God, our spiritual power grows, and we have the ability to resist the devil and rule over our natural desires.

Are these traits found in you in abundance? Are you filled with, and motivated by, the love of God? Are you led by the Spirit of God, doing only those things that are pleasing to Him? Are you putting to death the control of your life by the desires of the flesh? Invite the Holy Spirit to guide your life. Allow Him to direct everything that you do. Let Him lead you into all truth.

Jesus said that God's Word is truth. He also said, "It is the spirit that quickeneth; the flesh profiteth nothing: the words that I speak unto you, they are spirit, and they are life. But there are some of you that believe not…" (John 6:63–64).

When your spirit leaves your body, the body dies. The word "quickeneth" means to make alive. Spiritual words affect people spiritually. Some words cause love to be produced in those who hear them. Some words can cause hate to grow in those who hear them. If we have on the armor of God, we can be protected from the effects of evil words.

Some words can cause faith in those who hear them. Some words can produce fear in those who hear them—those who do not have the armor of God in place. Some words can produce peace in those who receive them.

What words produce in people is controlled by the condition of the ground of their heart. If they are good ground, good words about the kingdom of God will produce good results. Is your heart soft? Will you allow persecution, the cares of this life, or the deceitfulness of riches to make God's Word unfruitful in your life?

Do you view the Bible as the Word of God, or as fables made up by men? Do you believe that God exists and that He rewards those who diligently seek Him? All of creation tells us that there is a creator, but do you really believe in Him?

If you believe that the Bible is God's Word, it comes from a trustworthy source. Paul said to the Galatians that they received his words as the words of God, and he said that in fact they were God's words. They received Paul as a man sent from Almighty God with a message from Him.

As we taught in the chapter about the sower and the seed, if their heart was hard, shallow, or filled with the cares of this life, the Word would not have produced fruit in their lives.

Our ability to distinguish truth is based on our knowledge of truth. If we do not know anything on a given subject, we are open to believe everything that we hear about that subject. As we are taught, we develop beliefs that may or may not be based on truth. As children, we naturally believe everything that we are told until we encounter stronger evidence that is able to convince us that what we have already come to believe is false.

Adults often play games with children, lying to them and laughing at their inability to distinguish truth from lies. This is a terrible thing to do that begins to damage the child's ability to believe. It also teaches the child to lie, as if it were a good thing to produce pleasure.

As we demonstrated earlier, those who derive pleasure from evil are not filled with the love of God. Most of the children of this world are not raised in the truth of God's Word, but they are raised in an atmosphere of continual bombardment of lies and unbelief. They grow up confused and disoriented, filled with lies and evil desires.

The only guaranteed standard of truth in this world is the Word of God. It is the standard by which everything else must be judged. Without knowing the scriptures or the power of God, we are not qualified to judge any moral question.

Of whom [Jesus] we have many things to say, and hard to be uttered, seeing ye are dull of hearing. For when for the time ye ought to be teachers, ye have need that one teach you again which be the first principles of the oracles of God; and are become such as have need of milk, and not of strong meat. For every one that useth milk is

unskillful in the word of righteousness: for he is a babe. But strong
meat belongeth them that are of full age, even those who by reason
of use have their senses exercised to discern both good and evil.

HEBREWS 5:11–14

The writer is addressing those who have been around God's
Word for a long time, and yet do not have a very good understanding of it. He states that they ought to be teaching others by
now, but they still need someone to teach them the basic things of
God's Word. They have not studied to show themselves approved
unto God. Maybe they have not been good ground for the seed
of God's Word. Therefore, they lack the ability to really discern
between good and evil. They need someone to take them by the
hand and teach them the basics again. If they are too proud to
admit their ignorance, they will stay in that condition.

The Bible states that God resists the proud, but gives grace to
the humble (James 4:6). If we are too proud to realize that what
we believe is simply what we perceive to be true, we will not truly
consider information that is new to us. What we believe is not
true simply because we believe it. The information that we have
been given may be faulty. Many people interpret or teach what
they perceive God's Word to be saying.

I hope that I have encouraged you to study God's Word
intently to see if the things that I say are correct or not. I would
ask you to pray for God to give you the spirit of wisdom and
understanding. I pray that you will present your bodies as living
sacrifices to the God of heaven and earth, and that the fruit of the
Spirit will be evident in everything that you think, say, and do.

So what should our attitude be? We will discuss this in the
next chapter.

CHAPTER TEN

STAYING ON THE WAY
TO THE END

IF WE HAVE examined our lives and find the fruit of the Spirit in abundance and the works of the flesh are nonexistent, how should we think of ourselves? Paul discusses this subject in Philippians, chapter 3.

> But what things were gain to me, those I counted loss for Christ. Yea doubtless, and I count all things but loss for the excellency of the knowledge of Christ Jesus my Lord: for whom I have suffered the loss of all things, and do count them but dung, that I may win Christ, And be found in him, not having mine own righteousness, which is of the law, but that which is through the faith of Christ, the righteousness which is of God by faith: That I may know him, and the power of his resurrection, and the fellowship of his sufferings, being made conformable unto his death.
>
> PHILIPPIANS 3:7-10

Everything that was important to Paul (being circumcised the eighth day, an Israelite, of the tribe of Benjamin, a Hebrew of Hebrews, a Pharisee, persecuting the church, and blameless in matters of the law), he counted as dung compared to the value of knowing Christ Jesus, so that he might be justified by faith instead of the works of the law. (Being circumcised, keeping the feasts, bringing the sacrifices, not eating anything "unclean," washing of the hands, and other things according to tradition, and other matters of the sacrificial law.) This was so that he might know the power that raised Jesus from the dead (holiness, Romans 1:14); the sufferings of Jesus that made Him perfect or complete (Hebrews 2:10); and how to give his own life in the service of Jesus, as Jesus gave His life for us. All of this was done for one reason. Philippians 3:11 states: "If by any means I might attain unto the resurrection of the dead."

The purpose of all this sacrifice was to gain eternal life by the resurrection of the dead. Holiness was what gave Jesus resurrection from the dead. The wages of sin is death. The holiness that comes as a gift from God, and the ability to maintain it that comes from God, produce eternal life. This holiness that comes from giving your life to Christ and living for Him produces eternal life. "Follow peace with all men, and holiness, without which no man shall see the Lord" (Hebrews 12:14). This holiness, living without sin, is an absolute requirement to see God. Jesus compared holiness to light, because holiness exposes the evil in others around it.

Jesus said that the light came into the world, but men hated the light because their deeds were evil (John 3:19). Jesus was hated because His holiness made it apparent that those who claimed to be holy were evil. Jesus suffered and died, even for those who killed Him. This act of obedience assured Him a place at the right hand of the Father as King of kings and Lord of lords. Paul reached for holiness by losing everything that had been important to him for the sake of Christ Jesus.

> Not as though I had already attained, either were already perfect: but I follow after, if that I may apprehend that for which also I am apprehended of Christ Jesus. Brethren, I count not myself to have apprehended: but this one thing I do, forgetting those things which are behind, and reaching forth unto those things which are before, I press toward the mark for the prize of the high calling of God in Christ Jesus.
>
> PHILIPPIANS 3:12-14

Paul makes it clear that he is not claiming to be perfect, but a life of holiness is what Jesus called him to so that he might gain eternal life; that is, an immortal body to live in. He confesses and forgets his mistakes so he can focus on pressing toward the mark for the prize of the call to a holy life from God.

Second Corinthians 6:17–18 states: "Wherefore come out from among them, and be ye separate, saith the Lord, and touch not the unclean thing; and I will receive you, And will be a Father unto you, and ye shall be my sons and daughters, saith the Lord Almighty."

We are called to be holy as God is holy, so that we can be a member of the family of God. We cannot be like the other people in the world and still be a member of the family of God. We must learn from our mistakes, repent, and seek to be the person that God has called us to be. We cannot allow ourselves to mourn our mistakes, but we must get over them and move forward.

In the very next verse, Paul declares that everyone who is perfect, (complete, mature, grown up in Christ), should view themselves as not having already attained, but pressing toward the mark. In 1 Corinthians 10:12 he warns, "Wherefore let him that thinketh he standeth take heed lest he fall." When we think that we have become all that God requires, we are set up for a fall. This is not to put us in fear or doubt, but to keep us pressing toward the mark.

In Philippians, he continues by warning us not to let things slip that we have mastered, and to notice others who are living a real Christian life. He acknowledges that many Christians live as enemies of the cross of Christ, and that their reward will be eternity in the lake of fire. Their belly is their god. Their main motivation in life is to make a living, or to provide food for their stomach. They mind or take care of earthly things. They spend their time, attention, and effort securing the needs and desires of their body (Philippians 3:18–19).

This is not to say that they do not work, but their motivation for working is not to make a living. They work where God desires them to work, doing what God desires them to do, in the way God desires them to do it. They are directed by the Holy Spirit in all of these things. Their faith that comes from obedience sets them free from fear or concern over their needs. They are set free to serve God.

Our citizenship is in heaven, and our affection is set on heavenly things, not on earthly things (fun, partying, cars, toys, houses, clothes, business, animals, nature, or other earthly things). We do not desire the things of this life, because as citizens of heaven and Christ's kingdom we are strangers and aliens in the earth (Colossians 3:1–3, Philippians 3:20–21). This earth is no longer our home if we really are Christ's and citizens of the kingdom of heaven.

We cannot be wrapped up in sports, in love with business and making money, or wrapped up in any other earthly thing. Our desires have become the same as Christ's. We are focused on the things of God.

Many times Jesus advised us to count the cost. Search your heart to see if you are really willing to pay the price.

Luke 14:25–26 states: "And there went great multitudes with him: and he turned, and said unto them, If any man come to me, and hate not his father, and mother, and wife, and children, and brethren, and sisters, yea, and his own life also, he cannot be my disciple."

Pleasing Jesus must be more important to us than even life itself. This is the price to gain Christ and all the benefits of being found in Him, not having our own righteousness (established by bringing the right sacrifices at the proper time and keeping the other requirements of the sacrificial law), but trusting in the sacrifice of Jesus to pay the price for our sin. We place all of our faith and trust in Jesus in all things and at all times, especially faith that if we keep His commandments, we will attain eternal life. Jesus gave two illustrations to show the reason for this level of commitment.

Luke 14:28–30 states: "For which of you, intending to build a tower, sitteth not down first, and counteth the cost, whether he have sufficient to finish it? Lest haply, after he hath laid the foundation, and is not able to finish it, all that behold it begin to mock him, Saying, This man began to build, and was not able to finish."

This man began a big building project, but because he failed to count the cost before starting, he ran out of resources before the job was done. The result was wasted resources, an incomplete building, and the insulting laughter of everyone who passed by. He made a fool of himself. Those who claim to be Christian, but do not live the life, are ridiculed and scorned by those who observe them. Even ministry leaders are not immune to this.

Luke 14:34–35 states: "Salt is good: but if the salt have lost his savour, wherewith shall it be seasoned? It is neither fit for the land, nor yet for the dunghill: but men cast it out. He that hath ears to hear, let him hear."

If we do not pay the price and we do not live the life, those who observe us will not see the character of God that shows the world the nature of God. They will not see the real Jesus in us. If we are motivated by the same things as the rest of the world (lust of the flesh, lust of the eyes, and the pride of life), we will not show the character of God to the world.

Count the cost. The benefit is eternal life. Is any cost too high? Give your life totally to Jesus today. Begin today to press toward the mark. Do not become weary in following the commandments of Jesus. Jesus said, "But he that shall endure unto the end, the same shall be saved" (Matthew 24:13). We must be true to Christ to the end to be saved.

CHAPTER ELEVEN

WHAT IS "BORN AGAIN"?

There was a man of the Pharisees, named Nicodemus, a ruler of the Jews: The same came to Jesus by night, and said unto him, Rabbi, we know that thou art a teacher come from God: for no man can do these miracles that thou doest, except God be with him. Jesus answered and said unto him, Verily, verily, I say unto thee, Except a man be born again, he cannot see the kingdom of God. Nicodemus saith unto him, How can a man be born when he is old? can he enter the second time into his mother's womb, and be born? Jesus answered, Verily, verily, I say unto thee, Except a man be born of water and of the Spirit, he cannot enter into the kingdom of God. That which is born of the flesh is flesh; and that which is born of the Spirit is spirit. Marvel not that I said unto thee, Ye must be born again. The wind bloweth where it listeth, and thou hearest the sound thereof, but canst not tell whence it cometh, and whither it goeth: so is every one that is born of the Spirit.

JOHN 3:1-8

NICODEMUS WAS A PHARISEE. The Pharisees put forth as much effort to become what they believed God wanted them to be as anyone who has ever lived. They were extremely serious about their religion. Being carnal in nature, as we all are naturally, they attempted to accomplish this by dealing with a lot of rules that they made.

Their rules were called the "tradition of the elders." These laws governed every area of life. They covered what to eat, how to eat, who to eat with, what to wear, what to say, and an almost endless number of other things. They were extremely zealous in the performance of their religion (Romans 10:12). Their flaw was that what they did was not according to knowledge. In other words, they were not smart in how they went about striving to become the people that God desired them to be.

Paul, who was a Pharisee like Nicodemus, said, "For I through the law am dead to the law, that I might live unto God" (Galatians 2:19). The law convinced Paul that he could not live unless he gave his life to God. He stopped trying to gain eternal life by doing all of the right religious things and began living for God.

Galatians 2:20 states: "I am crucified with Christ: nevertheless I live; yet not I, but Christ liveth in me: and the life which I now live in the flesh I live by the faith of the Son of God, who loved me, and gave himself for me."

He died, yet he was still alive, for now Jesus' life was lived through Paul. Paul did not live to do what he personally desired; Paul lived to do what Jesus desired. He was motivated to do this because of the love of Jesus that was demonstrated on the cross. After he gave his life to Jesus, he was made into the person that he really desired to be as a Pharisee, and that is a person who pleases God.

Romans 8:3–4 states: "For what the law could not do, in that it was weak through the flesh, God sending his own Son in the likeness of sinful flesh, and for sin, condemned sin in the flesh: That the righteousness of the law might be fulfilled in us, who walk not after the flesh, but after the Spirit."

God condemned sin in the flesh. That means God said that sin in the flesh would cease to exist, so that we who live our lives being led by the Spirit might be pleasing to God. The righteous requirements of the law are kept in the lives of those who mind spiritual things.

The unselfish act of giving our lives to Jesus, motivated by our love for Jesus, produces the unselfish nature of God in us. Then the true nature of God is seen in us by those around us. This happens in response to the drawing of the Holy Spirit. When we feel the Holy Spirit drawing us to give our lives to Jesus and we respond by surrendering our lives to Him, this is the first step in being born again. This is being conceived by the Holy Spirit, just as a baby is conceived in its mother's womb. Life begins at conception, but the baby is not yet born.

The three parts of becoming a Christian are to deny yourself, take up your cross, and follow Jesus. The nature of God is found in us when we deny our flesh the opportunity to control our life. Then we surrender our life to Christ and we live in His Word so that we may be transformed into His likeness.

First John 3:9 states: "Whosoever is born of God doth not commit sin; for his seed remaineth in him: and he cannot sin, because he is born of God."

To be born of the Spirit is to be changed from selfish to unselfish. It is embodied in the giving of one's life to Christ so that we do not live for our own benefit any longer, but for God's.

Being born of water is being transformed by the renewing of the mind (Romans 12:2). It is being clean by the washing of the water of the Word (John 15:3; Ephesians 5:26). It is "being born again, not of corruptible seed, but of incorruptible, by the word of God, which liveth and abideth for ever" (1 Peter 1:23).

Until the spiritual birth takes place, the teachings of Jesus cannot be received. People who have not surrendered their lives to the lordship of Jesus do not submit to His commandments. We only obey those whom we accept as having authority over our lives. This only gives us the ability to believe that God's law is just and correct. Faith is required to live following Jesus' commandments.

If asked to go a mile, faith enables us to go two. If we are sued at the law, faith enables us to give more than is asked of us. If we are hit on one cheek, faith enables us to turn the other. Faith enables us to take no thought, saying, "What shall we have to eat, or what shall we drink?"

When the Lord told me to write this chapter, He told me to study Jacob's experience of wrestling with a man all night in Genesis 32. I studied this passage for at least a month and really got no satisfaction. I studied every reference to Jacob in the Bible. I read commentaries on this passage. I asked other students of the Bible. I asked pastors on the staff at my church. I learned a lot about Jacob, but I really could not see what the Holy Spirit was trying to teach me about this passage. Finally, after about a month of this, I told my wife that I was going into our closet to pray until the Lord told me what was going on with Jacob.

I prayed in tongues for about twenty minutes, not one word in English. Then the Holy Spirit spoke these words to me at least ten times in a row, "There's always travail with a birth!"

The next day I was led to read Galatians 4:19, which says, "My little children, of whom I travail in birth again until Christ be formed in you." *The Amplified Bible* says, "My little children, for whom I am again suffering birth pangs until Christ is completely and permanently formed (molded) within you" (Galatians 4:19, AMP).

This was written to church members. They had believed, been baptized, received the Holy Spirit, and had miracles performed in their church. But in Galatians 4:11 Paul states, "I am afraid of you, lest I have bestowed upon you labour in vain." In other words, he said that he feared for them, and that after he had spent so much time preaching, teaching, and writing to these people, they would turn from the gospel and become castaways.

There is always tremendous pain and trauma with a natural childbirth. The Lord said that there was always travail with a birth. Someone has to go through that pain. There is travail in putting to death the works of the flesh. Your flesh can scream at you when it does not get what it wants.

Jacob wrestled with God all night. When the Lord saw that He did not prevail against Jacob, he crippled Jacob. After that the Lord told Jacob to let Him go because the dawn was coming. Jacob replied that he would not let Him go until He blessed him.

Then the Lord asked Jacob what his name was. He replied that it was Jacob. The Lord declared that he would no longer be called Jacob, but he would be called "Israel" from that point forward; Jacob had power with God and with men like a prince, and he had prevailed.

Then Jacob asked Him what His name was. The Lord replied, "Wherefore is it that thou dost ask after my name?" (Genesis 32:29). Jacob called the place "Peniel," which means the face of God, because he said, "for I have seen God face to face, and my life is preserved" (Genesis 32:30).

The Lord allows trials and troubles to come to us to see if we will die in the womb (curse God and die, or simply turn loose of Him), or if we will overcome and endure to the end. If we hold on to the Lord to the end, in spite of anything that happens to us, we can be blessed at the end of the night (this life). All through this life we struggle with men and with God, but we must overcome as Jesus overcame to have life.

In the letters to the churches in Revelation 2 and 3, Jesus says to each church, "To him that overcometh." The first reward for overcoming is "to eat of the tree of life, which is in the midst of the paradise of God" (Revelation 2:7). The first promise is eternal life.

The second promise is, "Shall not be hurt of the second death" (Revelation 2:11). This is escaping the "lake of fire" (Revelation 20:14).

The third promise is, "Will I give to eat of the hidden manna, and will give him a white stone, and in the stone a new name written, which no man knoweth saving he that receiveth it" (Revelation 2:17). When the children of Israel escaped from Egypt (the world), they were sustained by the perfect food (manna) from God. In the ancient world when a person was declared not guilty in court, he was given a white stone. Just as the Lord gave Jacob a new name, He gives us a new character like His own. This determination of not guilty comes after we have overcome and endure to the end.

The fourth promise is, "He that overcometh, and keepeth my works unto the end, to him will I give power over the nations: And he shall rule them with a rod of iron; as the vessels of a potter shall they be broken to shivers: even as I received of my Father. And I will give him the morning star" (Revelation 2:26–28). Those who lose their heads for the testimony of Jesus during the Great Tribulation will rule the nations with Christ for a thousand years (Revelation 20:4). Christ Jesus is the bright and morning star, and these gain the right to reign with Him for a thousand years.

The fifth promise is, "The same shall be clothed in white raiment; and I will not blot out his name out of the book of life, but I will confess his name before my Father, and before his angels" (Revelation 3:5). These will be clothed in purity and will receive eternal life. Their holiness is shown by their white robes, and that holiness gives them eternal life. Once again, this is for those who endure to the end.

The sixth promise is, "Him that overcometh will I make a

pillar in the temple of my God, and he shall go no more out: and I will write upon him the name of my God, and the name of the city of my God, which is new Jerusalem, which cometh down out of heaven from my God: and I will write upon him my new name" (Revelation 3:12).

David said that he desired one thing, and that was that he could dwell in the house of God all the days of his life. These people are made a permanent fixture in the house of God forever, and they are marked as belonging to God, to His city, and to the King of kings.

The seventh promise is, "To him that overcometh will I grant to sit with me in my throne, even as I also overcame, and am set down with my Father in his throne" (Revelation 3:21). This is the ultimate. It is better than sitting on His right hand. This is being invited to sit in the boss' seat. It does not get any better than this. How do we get there? It is given "to him that overcometh."

Life begins at conception, but our life is counted as beginning at birth. Likewise, we have life when we are born of the Spirit, but our eternal life begins after we overcome and endure to the end.

We wrestle with, "Be ye therefore perfect, even as your Father which is in heaven is perfect" (Matthew 5:48). It is one thing to be good in the opinion of people, but it is a different thing to be holy as God is holy. If this is required, we respond like the disciples and ask, "Who then can be saved?" (Matthew 19:25).

Jesus gave us the answer, "With men this is impossible; but with God all things are possible" (Matthew 19:26). How is this accomplished in our lives?

To obtain eternal life, we must love the Lord our God more than our life, and our neighbor as ourselves. We must endure the travail that comes to us in this life and endure to the end.

Just as the children of Israel came out of Egypt (the world) by passing through the Red Sea (the blood of Jesus) and came into the wilderness (living in this world without being of this world), we also find ourselves in the wilderness. We live by faith, depending on the Lord for everything and praying, "Give us this day our daily bread." Just as the Israelites received a day's supply of manna each day, except on the sixth day each week when they received two day's supply, we stay dependent on the Lord throughout this life.

As we continue going through the travail of this life, we are tested over and over again. This is to see if we can overcome as Jesus overcame. James said that the testing of our faith would produce patience, which would make us complete and entire, lacking nothing. Then we will be equipped for any assignment that the Lord may have for us.

As this age comes to a close, the travail of the kingdom of God being birthed into this world will increase greatly to the point to where it is called the Great Tribulation. In Matthew 24 Jesus said that wars and rumors of wars were the beginning of this travail. It will intensify to the point where a third of everything that draws breath on the earth will die during this period.

This travail is an effort on God's part to convince the people of the world to repent. Jesus said that this travail will be so strong that no flesh—that is, any being who has flesh—will survive this period if those days are not stopped. Will you survive that travail with your faith intact, or will you die in the womb?

Jacob wrestled with God all night, and then the Lord said to Jacob, "Let me go!" After we have wrestled with the Lord, the cry goes out at midnight, "The bridegroom cometh!" Will you have oil in your lamp? Will your light still shine?

Will you count the cost and give yourself totally to Jesus today? The cost is not too high.

My prayer for you is this: "The Lord bless thee, and keep thee: The Lord make his face shine upon thee, and be gracious unto thee: The Lord lift up his countenance upon thee, and give thee peace" (Numbers 6:24–26).

BIBLIOGRAPHY

1. *The Amplified New Testament,* La Habra, California: The Lockman Foundation, 1958, 1987.
2. *The Holy Bible, Authorized King James Version,* Nashville, Tennessee: Holman Bible Publishers, 1982.
3. *The Holy Bible, New International Version,* New York, New York: International Bible Society, 1978.
4. *Webster's Seventh New Collegiate Dictionary,* Springfield, Massachusetts: G&C Merriam Company, 1970.